PRACTICE AND REALIZATION

PRACTICE AND REALIZATION
STUDIES IN KANT'S MORAL PHILOSOPHY

by

NATHAN ROTENSTREICH

1979

MARTINUS NIJHOFF

THE HAGUE / BOSTON / LONDON

Library of Congress Cataloging in Publication Data   CIP

Rotenstreich, Nathan, 1914–
    Practice and realization.

    Includes bibliographical references and indexes.
    1.   Kant, Immanuel, 1724–1804 – Ethics.   2.   Ethics.   3.   Practice (Philosophy)   I.
    Title.
    B2799.E8R67   1979   170'.92'4   78–31393

ISBN 90–247–2112–1

© *1979 by Martinus Nijhoff Publishers bv, The Hague.*
All rights reserved. No part of this publication
may be reproduced, stored in a retrieval system, or
transmitted in any form or by any means, mechanical,
photocopying, recording, or otherwise, without the
prior written permission of the publisher, Martinus
Nijhoff Publishers bv, P.O.B. 566, 2501 CN The Hague, The Netherlands.

PRINTED IN THE NETHERLANDS

TABLE OF CONTENTS

PREFACE

The present book is an exploration of some basic issues of Kant's moral philosophy. The point of departure is the concept of freedom and the self-legislation of reason. Since self-legislation is expressed in the sphere of practice or morality, it is meant to overcome some of the vulnerable aspects of Kant's theoretical philosophy, namely that which Kant himself pointed to and called the 'lucky chance,' in so far as the application of reason to sensuous data is concerned.

The book attempts to show that Kant's practical or moral philosophy faces questions which are parallel to those he faced in the sphere of his theoretical philosophy. The problematic situation of realization of practice is parallel to the problematic situation of application of theory. It is in the line of the problems emerging from Kant's practical philosophy that the present book deals with some of Kant's minor writings, or less-known ones, including his writings in the sphere of politics, history and education. The limitations of self-legislation – this is the theme of the book. The book is parallel to the author's previous one on Kant: 'Experience and its Systematization – Studies in Kant" (Nijhoff, 1965, 2nd edition 1973), as well as to: "From Substance to Subject – Studies in Hegel" (Nijhoff, 1974).

Jerusalem 1978

ABBREVIATIONS

As to the references to Kant's major works, the following procedure will be observed: *Kritik der reinen Vernunft* will be quoted as *Kr.d.r.V.*, with the number of the page. After the semicolon (;) the reference will be to Immanuel Kant's *Critique of Pure Reason*, translated by Norman Kemp-Smith, New York, St. Martin's Press, Toronto, Macmillan, 1965. The number will refer to the page in that edition. *Kritik der praktischen Vernunft* is referred to as *Kr.d.p.V.* in Karl Vorländer's edition, Felix Meiner in Leipzig, 1929. After the semicolon (;) the number refers to the page in Immanuel Kant, *Critique of Practical Reason*, translated with an introduction by Lewis White Beck, New York, The Liberal Arts Press, 1956. *Kritik der Urteilskraft* will be referred to *Kr.d.U.* in Karl Vorländer's edition, Felix Meiner in Leipzig, 1924. After the semicolon (;) the reference will be to the pages in Immanuel Kant: *The Critique of Judgment*, Translated with Analytical Indexes by James Creed Meredith, Oxford, at the Clarendon Press, 1964. This edition has two parts, each of which with separate pagination. The reference will be to the volume (I, II) and to the pages.

The smaller writings of Kant's will be quoted in their English translations in so far as they are available. Some of the smaller writings appear in: *Immanuel Kant on History*, edited with an introduction by Lewis Beck, translated by Lewis White Beck, Robert E. Anchor and Emil L. Fackenheim, Indianapolis, N.Y., The Library of Liberal Arts, the Bobbs-Merrill Company, 1963. The references will be to the individual essays; *On History* will signify that volume.

Kant's other works will be quoted as follows: *Anthropologie in pragmatischer Hinsicht*, Herausgegeben und erläutert von J.H. von Kirchmann, Berlin, Verlag von L. Heimann 1869 – as *Anthropologie*. *Immanuel Kants Metaphysik der Sitten*, Herausgegeben und erläutert von J.H. von Kirchmann, Leipzig, Verlag der Dürr'schen Buchhandlung, 1870 – as *Met.d.S.* *Religion within the Limits of Reason alone*, translated with a introduction and notes by Theodore M. Greene and Hoyt Hundson, with a new essay "The Ethical Significance of Kant's *Religion*" by John R. Silver, New York and Evanston, Harper & Row, 1960 – as *Religion*.

The various other writings of Kant will be quoted as indicated in the respective footnotes.

CHAPTER ONE

FREEDOM, ACTION AND DEEDS

1

It is an established fact that Kant's theory of deeds or acts can ultimately be equaled with his ethical theory. This needs to be said at the outset since there are in Kant traces of the classical and medieval distinction between *praxis* and *poiesis*. The medieval rendering of this distinction as that between *actio immanens* and *actio transiens* is an even more suitable point of departure for the attempt to understand the direction of Kant's theory and some of its problems than that between *praxis* and *poiesis*. *Actio immanens* connotes an action which remains within the sphere of the agent or, conversely, which produces no outcome other than the action itself. *Actio transiens* on the other hand is an action which has an effect beyond the agent and which comes to be embodied in a product, like a house or ship. Kant's version on the notion of *actio immanens* can be summarized as an attempt to develop this basic concept. It is not enough for the action to remain within its own boundaries. As an ethical action it has to emerge from the motivation and commands of reason or, conversely, it cannot be determined by causes outside the scope of reason and of its influence on the agent. For Kant therefore *actio immanens* comes to be consonant with free action. We are about to discuss some of the features of this theory, but it is necessary to begin with a broader treatment of some of the concepts Kant uses with reference to the sphere of action, like "*Handlung*," "*Tätigkeit*," "pragmatical," "practical."

The distinction between *activum* and *factivum* is parallel to that between *actio immanens* and *actio transiens*. *Activum* is an operation initiated by the subject which perfects him. Thinking, willing and sensing (*intelligere, velle, sentire*) are operations listed under the heading of *activum*. *Factivum* on the other hand produces artifacts outside the agent. Placing the emphasis, as it does, on the origin of activity and its immanent outcome, Kant's theory of ethics is a version of *activum*, although he would clearly not list *sentire* among immanent activities. Insofar as medieval philosophy attributed qualities of action to God, it attributed *intelligere* and *velle* to Him, and not, naturally enough, *sentire* which comprised hearing and seeing – *audire* and *videre*. Kant's theory of spontaneity and its impact on ethics and action is indeed a version of *intelligere* and *velle*.[1]

2

Let us begin with the definition of action which appears in the *Critique of Pure Reason:* "Action signifies the relation of the subject of causality to its effect."[2] It is apparent from this definition that the concept of the subject is essential for action and that this concept can legitimately be interpreted as the agent or carrier of the action. Moreover, action is a kind of causality, for action brings about an effect and an effect, as Kant subsequently says, is that which happens. Action can be listed under the broad heading of the transition from not-being of a state of affairs to being of a state of affairs.[3]

When we confine our attention to human deeds, we are bound to come across the distinction between empirical conduct and the intelligible cause of volition and action or that between phenomenal appearance and expression and its noumenal character. In spite of the fact that they are human actions, phenomenal expressions have to be accounted for in the same manner as all other natural appearances, namely in conformity with unchangeable laws.[4] As regards the empirical character and its actions, there is no freedom. Freedom can be viewed as a causality or as a cause of action only insofar as actions are conceived in their relation to reason. Kant introduces a complication here in that he does not refer here to speculative reason, whose task is to explain how actions come into being, but refers to reason as a cause of action – in this sense combining the notion of the practical with that of reason as a cause.[5] The shift from actions determined in the causal sequence to actions produced by reason leads to the conclusion that, since reason is not subject to the conditions of sensibility, its position as a cause

---

[1] Consult: Francis Nugent, Immanent Action in St. Thomas and Aristotle, *The New Scholasticism*, vol. XXVII, 1963, p. 164ff.

Kant describes the ethical lawgiving as one which can not be external and belongs to the internal sphere. The juridical lawgiving can be external too. External in the sense implied here connotes an external act not accompanied by inner conviction; hence the notion of external does not carry the meaning of transiens. But the notion of inner or internal is very close indeed to that of immanens. See: *Metaphysik der Sitten*, p. 20.

[2] *Kr.d.r.V.*, p. 250; p. 229.

[3] *Ibid.*, p. 251; p. 230.

[4] *Ibid.*, p. 826; p. 631.

[5] *Ibid.*, p. 578; p. 474.

cannot be lodged in any time sequence. The dynamical law of nature, which determines succession in time in accordance with rules, is not applicable to reason; hence it is not applicable to reason as a cause either.[6] The problem which Kant faced here is that of specifying the status of reason as a cause or as having causality. His wording is perhaps more cautious than the real direction of his thought. He says that the fact that our reason has causality is evident from the imperatives, and that these impose rules upon our active powers in all matters of conduct.[7] The sphere of imperatives or that of the "ought" (*das Sollen*) is a dimension beyond nature, since we cannot say that anything in nature ought to be other than it actually is. We can ask questions such as 'what happens about nature," but we cannot commend something to happen. Hence the notion of the "ought" expresses a possible action, whose ground cannot be anything but a concept or reason which, by its very position and essence, does not follow the order of things; it frames an order of its own, in accordance with ideas.[8] This part of the investigation of Kant's vocabulary and its background can be summarized by saying that the term "action" is now subdivided into two spheres: action as a mere event or effect, or as the cause of an effect, and action as grounded in an imperative. Practical philosophy has to do with the second mode of action; the immanent character of action indicated earlier now gives it the form of an action whose cause is reason. Only an action of this kind can be immanent in the strict sense of the term.

The concept of the "practical" has already been introduced. Kant says in another context that the function of prescribing laws by means of the concept of freedom is discharged by reason and is merely practical.[9] But he superimposes the distinction between that which is technically-practical and that which is morally-practical on the distinction between being and ought, or nature and reason. He lists rules of art and skill, or even those of prudence as the skill of exercising an influence over men and their wills under technically-practical rules. The rules we are referring to here are not physical laws, but only precepts; they are still not practical rules in the strict sense in which the practical is identical with the moral, or in which the practical connotes rules grounded in reason. Technical precepts relate to man's natural motives or to the given situation in which human beings find themselves. That which is technically practical relates essentially to the skill of producing an effect which is possible in accordance with natural concepts of cause and effect.

---

[6] *Ibid.*, p. 581; p. 476.
[7] *Ibid.*, p. 575; p. 472.
[8] *Ibid.*, p. 575–576; p. 472–473.
[9] *Kr.d.U.*, p. 6; p. 12.

To paraphrase Kant's view, a technical-practical action is one which interferes in the natural course of action using natural causes to produce effects.[10] As opposed to these interventions of the practical, the legislative character of practical or morally-practical reason, has to be underlined.[11] The legislative character of the practical arises from the concept of freedom, since the concept of freedom is meant to actualize the end proposed by its laws in the sensible world. Again, while the technical use of a practical approach is meant to take advantage of natural events, the practical manifestation of reason in the moral sense is meant to establish a realm of its own and not merely utilize a given realm for its own objectives.

The distinction between the two modes of practicallity is to some extent coterminous with the distinction between that which is practical and that which is pragmatic. Kant relates the term "pragmatic" to the rules of prudence (*Klugheitsregeln*); which, as we have said is one of the skills embraced under the general heading of the technically-practical. It is valid to assume that pragmatic rules and laws refer not only to prudence in general but to prudence as motivated by the aspiration to achieve happiness.[12] Prudence coordinates the means of attaining happiness; but as usual in Kant – and we will come back to this – the aspiration to attain happiness is an attempt to attain the ends commended by the senses. Pragmatic considerations cannot therefore be related to reason and its legislative manifestations, for what is motivated by the senses cannot yield pure laws which are determined completely *a priori*. In this sense, the pragmatic application of prudence would only be an expression of the technical attitude and approach.[13]

A variation on the notion of the pragmatic attitude is the concept of pragmatic belief (*pragmatischer Glaube*). Kant's illustration of this kind of belief is derived from medicine: a physician must do something for a patient in danger, without knowing the nature of the patient's illness. His diagnosis is in his own estimation only a contingent belief. "Such contingent belief, which yet forms the ground for the actual employment of means to certain actions, I entitle *pragmatic belief*."[14] Here contingent belief is once more a form of prudence related to the natural course of events; illness is a state of the organism, and healing an interference in the process of the organism which takes advantage of the possibilities of nature's recuperative powers.

Yet Kant expands the concept of the pragmatic without losing sight of the

---

[10] *Ibid.*, p. 7; p. 9–11.
[11] *Ibid.*, p. 7; p. 13.
[12] *Kr.d.r.V.*, p. 834; p. 636.
[13] *Ibid.*, p. 828; p. 632.
[14] *Ibid.*, p. 852; p. 648.

fundamental distinction between the moral and the pragmatic. The pragmatic broadly connotes the principle of employing means for an end.[15] This juxtaposition would suggest that morality is, by definition, related to ends in the strict sense of the term, while the pragmatic employment of our powers is, by definition, only related to means. This obviously differs from the previous statement, where the pragmatic attitude implied an aspiration directed toward a specific end, namely to that of happiness, or implied lack of *a priori* certainty, as in the case of the doctor and his patient.

These qualifications do not yet exhaust the variety of the meanings attributed to the notion of the pragmatic in Kant's diverse writings. There is a kind of communal enlargement or amplification of happiness when Kant speaks of the general welfare. Here the "pragmatic" would mean that which belongs to the general welfare; pragmatic sanctions relate to concern for the general welfare (*Vorsorge für allgemeine Wohlfahrt*). Kant is probably coming back to one of the traditional ways of understanding the notion of the pragmatic here as well as to the *pragmatica sanctio*, which refers to the affairs of the community, though Kant may be adding the particular emphasis on the welfare of the community.

Yet Kant also uses the term "pragmatic history," not in the more widespread sense of interpreting history by exploring causes and effects, but in the sense of teaching human beings how to be prudent by attending to their advantage better than preceding generations, or at least no less than preceding generations.[16] In summary, then, there are actions according to the sequence of time controlled by the laws of nature and there are pragmatic actions related to prudence either in the individual sense or in the communal sense, though the notion of pragmatic still carries the traditional overtone of being shrewd or business-like. Kant suggests that to be shrewd is to care for one's advantage, and advantage belongs under the broad heading of happiness or welfare. Insofar as the pragmatic connotes prudence and refers to human beings, it is still a non-poetic action and an *actio immanens*, or it is human happiness rather than an artifact embodied in a material which is brought about by pragmatic considerations.

Systematically speaking we are facing here the distinction between the sensible and that which is grounded in reason, as well as the distinction between prudence and pragmatical considerations on the one hand and moral

---

[15] Verkündigung des nahen Abschlusses eines Traktats zum ewigen Frieden in der Philosophie, 1796, in *Immanuel Kants Werke*, ed. E. Cassirer, Bd. VI, Bruno Cassirer, 1914, p. 512.

[16] *The Moral Law or Kant's Groundwork of the Metaphysic of Morals*, transl. by H.J. Paton, New York, Melbourne etc., p. 84 note.

and practical considerations on the other. Whether this distinction can be maintained in a given human situation is not at all clear. Kant himself says the following: "The real morality of actions, their merit or guilt, even that of our own conduct, thus remains entirely hidden from us. Our imputations can refer only to the empirical character. How much of this character is ascribable to the pure effect of freedom, how much to mere nature, that is, to faults of temperament for which there is no responsibility, or to its happy constitution (*merito fortunae*), can never be determined; and upon it therefore no perfectly just judgments can be passed."[17] This statement which clearly expresses Kant's awareness of the difficulty of applying his systematic dichotomies, has to be elaborated in the context of Kant's reflections on history, education and groups of people as historical agents. But to understand Kant's dilemmas here it is necessary to understand some additional details of his notion of the practical.

3

As we have seen, Kant hesitates about the precise meaning of the concept of the "practical." The different attempts to define variations of the practical, like the distinction between technical and moral or the particular meaning of the pragmatic, suggest a separation of the practical from more diverse meanings in order to establish that it is synonymous with the moral. This separation is not completely unambiguous, or at least, it poses some significant problems in view of what Kant says, for instance, about practical concepts. In general they "relate to objects of satisfaction or dissatisfaction, that is, of pleasure and pain, and therefore, at least indirectly, to the objects of our feelings."[18] The question here is how the sphere of the practical, which essentially has a moral meaning in the singular sense of the term, can indicate objects of feelings, pleasure and pain, which do not have a moral character. One might even suggest that insofar as pleasure and pain are concerned, Kant should be speaking of the pragmatic rather than of the practical. It could be assumed that this is a vague expression, and that the practical stands for the pragmatic here. But perhaps a closer examination will show that there is something more significant involved: there is a dialectical relation between the practical and the object of our feelings.

The broad heading for an analysis of the practical in the strict sense of the term is the identity between the practical and the moral, and ultimately the

---

[17] *Kr.d.r.V.*, p. 579 note; p. 475 note.
[18] *Ibid.*, p. 830 note; p. 633 note.

identity between the practical and freedom. How these different angles of identification can be understood is indeed one of the central perplexities of the Kantian system. The sphere of the practical is by definition related to deeds. Deed (*Tat*), says Kant, is an action insofar as it is subject to laws of obligation (*Gesetze der Verbindlichkeit*).[19] This definition indicates an area of action which is characterized by its relation to moral laws, but their moral character has to be made explicit. We are no longer concerned with a variety of acts, but only with those which fulfil certain conditions. Whereas the traditional view of praxis tended to underline the shaping character of human emotions and attitudes, Kant emphasizes its subjection to laws. With reference to the previous quotation about practical concept and objects of feelings it could now be said that the sphere of the practical is that of deeds, which in turn lead from subjection to feelings of pain or pleasure to consent to and affirmation of the law. The sphere of praxis is essentially a sphere of tension between the impact of feelings and the guidance of laws of obligation. It is in this sense that Kant calls virtue (*Tugend*) the moral disposition in conflict, or respect for the moral law or for duty.[20] The conflict will result in a decision or option for the moral law in accordance with the imperative it imposes. Duty is an action to which one is obligated.[21] The imperative character of command or prohibition is amplified by the fact that imperatives do not directly or immediately conform to the direction of the will.[22] We can therefore summarize this part of our analysis by indicating that in Kant praxis as an act is an action in a clearly defined direction: it transcends the inherent tendency of the will by opting for a commandment. Kant reiterates that praxis is a choice of the will which transcends natural inclinations. He attempts to establish an identity between practice and morality from both ends: morality is in itself practical,[23] but at the same time practice is essentially morality. It is because of this double identity that Kant imposes a theory of ethics on the phenomenology of practice – and this is a major problematic issue in his system, as we shall try to show presently.

It is possible to go on to analyse the practical character of morality, once morality is understood as Kant understood it. The first, obvious, point is the reference of both practice and morality to will: "Practical principles are propositions which contain a general determination of the will ..." "As-

---

[19] *Met.d.S.*, p. 23.
[20] *Kr.d.p.V.*, p. 99; p. 87.
[21] *Met.d.S.*, p. 22; *ibid.*, p. 21.
[22] *Ibid.*, p. 21.
[23] *Eternal Peace. On History*, p. 117.

suming that pure reason can contain a practical ground sufficient to determine the will, then there are practical laws.''[24] It is therefore essential to
consider the essence of will first. Kant basically defines will in such a way as to
make it the promotor of an act of decision which conforms to the representation of an end. Though Kant places will in the broad sphere of the
faculty of desire (*Begehrungsvermögen*), he nevertheless emphasizes the subjection of desire to concepts or its determinability by concepts.[25] Thus from
the very beginning will ceases to be an exclusively activating factor and becomes a pre-established synthesis between being a mover and having a
certain direction. Since its direction is prescribed by concepts, Kant is bound
to view the very nature of the will as an implicit synthesis of desire and
concepts. In this sense, will as an essential ingredient of practice is already
a total *Gestalt* of practice qua morality, or at least a predisposition for
morality insofar as morality contains a determination of the will by laws
of pure reason. Yet the issue is still ambiguous, because Kant has to make
several distinctions or qualifications. He distinguishes between a purely
animal will which is a promoting agent that can only be determined by
sensuous impulses and free will which is determined by rational motives.
This is a clear concession to the existence of a will which is not *ab initio*
determined by concepts and which does not contain a synthesis of rules and
drives. Everything which is bound up with free will, whether as ground or
as consequence, is practical in the strict sense of the term.[26] In a sense the
very nature of the sphere of the practical demands a grounding in will, since
it is a sphere of action, and will represents the motivation for action or for
the agent. But the sphere of the practical nevertheless also indicates the relation of the reason to will.[27] We therefore have to ask to what extent reason
can be practical *per se* and not merely because of its synthesis with the will.
Again this is by no means a question with a clear or evident answer.

If reason is understood as the whole higher faculty of knowledge – there is
no indication of the practical direction reason can take. Even in a more
limited sense, when it is stated that reason never applies itself directly to
experience or to any object, it applies itself to understanding in order to
give the latter's manifold knowledge an *a priori* unity by means of concepts.
This unity is called the unity of reason.[28] Here, too, the unifying character
of reason or its meta-unity in comparison to the lower unity of understanding,

[24] *Kr.d.p.V.*, p. 21; p. 17.
[25] *Kr.d.U.*, p. 59; p. 61.
[26] *Kr.d.r.V.*, p. 830; p. 633.
[27] *Kr.d.r.V.*, p. 67; p. 58.
[28] *Kr.d.r.V.*, p. 359; p. 303.

neither contains the component of practicality which would turn pure reason into practical reason, nor presents pure reason as containing a practical component.

There are several possible attempts in Kant to include the practical aspect in pure reason. The most prominent and problematic of these is the notion of the tasks of pure reason or the ultimate aim of rational speculation concerning three objects – the freedom of will, the immortality of the soul, and the existence of God. All three have a bearing on the theory of morality, and the notion of the freedom of will is even a presupposition for the assessment of the intelligible cause of volition.[29] But here, too, a distinction has to be made between the reason which refers to objects like the freedom of will, the immortality of the soul and the existence of God, – and reason as such, which is imbued with the quality of freedom in the moral sense of the term, that is to say, which is an *a priori* synthesis of a certain manifestation of the faculty of desire and a certain end. In other words, we regard reason essentially as will, and as parallel to the structure of the free will which is essentially not only a desire but also reason. The question is whether Kant faced this central issue, or whether he perhaps used the term "practical reason", if we may venture this blasphemy, naively. Kant has to show that reason is practical and even that it can be employed practically. This again would call for a phenomenology of reason parallel to Kant's sporadic attempts to write a phenomenology of practice.

Within the scope of his systematic concepts Kant can say, and indeed does say, that reason is impelled by a tendency inherent in its nature to go beyond the field of its empirical employment. This tendency amounts to a venture in the direction of a pure employment by means of ideas only.[30] But our question is not related to the breakthrough characteristic of reason's inherent tendency, but to the synthesis between reason and will, or to the way this synthesis of the transcending character of reason and will comes about when reason provides the ends of desire, thus depriving the latter of its implication of animality. This is basically a circular argument: for will to be capable of absorbing the determination by reason it must be presupposed that reason has already deprived will of its sensuous determination, and also that will as a factor impelling to action, can in turn be a vehicle for the determination of reason because of the primordial affinity between the two. After all, reason might very well remain a self-contained faculty of principles without finding a sphere for its realization in a will capable of determination by concepts and ends, instead of being determined merely by desires. Kant

[29] *Ibid.*, p. 826; p. 631.
[30] *Ibid.*, p. 825; p. 630.

ultimately elevates the will and desire from empirical expressions to recep-
tacles for the determination by reason. Reason therefore, becomes practical
by determining will. Still, there is no built-in ground in reason for it to
become that determining factor, since reason determines will but will does
not emanate from reason. The very fact that will separates itself from the
sensuous determination and makes itself subject to rules and laws of reason
is not to be explained by describing the various manifestations of will.
Reason has to intervene in order to deprive will from sensuality and in order
to enable it to accept and absorb the impact of the laws of pure reason.
There is a leap from the day-to-day human reality to the plateau of will, and
then an attempt to create an all-embracing plateau of will and reason.

This basic difficulty in the concept of the practical and in its identity with
morality can be put differently: Pure reason as a faculty of principles creates
principles out of its own spontaneity. These principles become rules only
from the perspective of a factor or an agent to be ruled. This perspective is
one of will, which does not as such follow from the existence of spontaneity,
though Kant is led to assume that free will is a spontaneous will, and therefore contains a quality similar to the quality of reason. But even so, the
spontaneity of reason is one of formulation, while the spontaneity of will is
one of choice and direction. Hence the two aspects of spontaneity cannot be
identified in spite of Kant's attempt to make them identical, or at least akin.
The question of the emergence of demands, commandments and obedience
to demands cannot be avoided, for neither do demands follow analytically
from rules nor does obedience to demands derive analytically from demands
and their formulation.

One of the applications of the notion that the same reason manifests
itself both theoretically and practically is the emphasis placed by Kant on
the logical character of duty. This emphasis is only an explication of an
underlying notion that even pure reason is imbued with a logical structure
which can be discerned through formal logic. Many of Kant's statements
about the logical character of duty can be adduced here, but one of the most
radical is the statement about duty being grounded in the logical use of man's
reason; the specific reference is the duty to respect man.[31]

The identification of practice and morality, which is one of the results of
our analysis, presupposes a harmony between will and reason, but does not
establish that harmony or even argue for the possibility of maintaining it
discursively and analytically. Kant says: "The relation of such a will to this
law is one of dependence under the name of "obligation" (*Abhängigkeit –
Verbindlichkeit*). This term implies a constraint (*Nötigung*) to an action,

[31] *Met.d.S.*, p. 315 note.

though this constraint is only that of reason and its objective law."[32] There is again a basic lack of clarity here about the extent to which will is free in being determined by the law. If it is free then either it is not constrained by the affinity between will and reason, or the determination by reason is still a constraint, since will as such contains the capacity of moving in directions beyond those described by reason. And indeed Kant speaks of passive constraint, though the ground for moral constraint (*sittliche Verbindlichkeit*) lies *a priori* merely in concepts of pure reason. Obviously, passivity cannot be due to the existence of the concept of pure reason. It can only emerge in the context of the impact this concept has on human will, constraining the human will to create a situation of passive constraint (*passive Nötigung*) in spite of the fact that the will chooses what it ought to choose. Kant says that the counterpart of the metaphysics of morals would be moral anthropology. Moral anthropology would only contain the subjective conditions in human nature for the execution of the laws, both inhibitive and favourable.[33] But the question is whether Kant is providing an adequate exposition of the structure of his own system, when he says that moral anthropology is only a supplement to moral philosophy. After all, the very description of will presupposes the existence of human beings endowed with will. Will in its moral sense is one of the manifestations or formations of the will in its broad pragmatic or practical sense. Moreover, the very elevation of the will as an agent for the determination of the moral precepts presupposes a phenomenological structure which distinguishes between factors and objectives. This too is a feature of the anthropological situation, a feature which is given special meaning and direction in the area of moral philosophy. Passivity implies also a transformation of the passivity known to the empirical human subject whose awareness is to be studied in moral anthropology, though the passivity is now one of will and its relation to reason and not a fortuitous determination by circumstances or demands lacking a grounding in reason. The interaction between will and reason is essentially not a separation from the anthropological sphere but an elevation or sublimation of that sphere. The issue will now be reiterated in a closer analysis of the concept of freedom.

4

In an analysis of the concept of freedom, two questions come to the fore: to what extent is freedom essentially a phenomenon in the realm of practice

---

[32] *Kr.d.p.V.*, p. 38; p. 32.
[33] *Met.d.S.*, p. 16.

and is freedom as such an act or a deed? We begin our analysis by summarizing Kant's presentation of freedom.

In its cosmological meaning freedom is the power of beginning a state by itself (*von selbst*).[34] This definition of freedom can be called positive since it describes freedom as causality, causation or absolute self-activity.[35] This definition is close to St. Augustin who pointed out that there is fundamentally no will behind the will (*voluntas*); will as such contains in itself the very beginning. But there is a negative aspect in Kant's presentation too. Self-activity is juxtaposed with being governed by another cause which is lodged in time, and thus subject to the law of nature. Once the broad definition of freedom in the cosmological sense is transposed to the sphere of practicality and morality, lack of subjection to the laws of nature amounts to man's power of self-determination or lack of coercion by sensuous impulses.[36]

The aspect of the practical manifestation of freedom emphasized before in our analysis of will, recurs here: the lack of determination by sensibility amounts to the determination by reason, reason creating for itself a spontaneity which can begin to act of itself.[37] What is still unclear in the shift towards the determination by reason is whether that determination is an act of acknowledgement of reason or whether the spontaneity characteristic of the ability of will and reason's spontaneity guiding the initial spontaneity of will are identical. This could be reformulated with reference to the previous question relating to the phenomenon of will, since Kant speaks of the will's independence of coercion from sensuous impulses. To put it differently, it is necessary to ask whether there are two levels of spontaneity, that characteristic of freedom as an initiator, and that characteristic of reason guiding the ability to initiate on objectively determinable grounds. Kant refers to reason in the second sense in Prolegomena, paragraph 53: reason is always free, since reason cannot by definition be determined by sensuality. This question is even more articulate when referred to the notion of spontaneity. Kant speaks of absolute spontaneity of the cause: a series of appearances proceeding in accordance with the laws of nature is self-generated. But it is obvious that spontaneity is not confined to freedom as the ability to initiate an act, since spontaneity is characteristic of understanding or of cognitive performance in general – it is the mind's ability to produce presentations

---

[34] *Kr.d.r.V.*, p. 561; p. 464. The English translation reads here: spontaneously.
[35] *Ibid.*, p. 446; p. 392.
[36] *Ibid.*, p. 562; p. 465.
[37] *Ibid.*, p. 561; p. 465.

from itself.[38] The *tertium comparationis* between freedom as spontaneity and the spontaneity of knowledge would lie in the mind's (*Gemüt*) ability to produce representations – in one case in the direction of acts, in the second in the direction of representations. But granting this, the distinction between acts and representations would have to be a distinction which precedes the assessment of their common source of origin in spontaneity. Hence the practical direction would have a sort of independence guiding spontaneity, as the cognitive direction would have a kind of independence in channelling spontaneity in the direction of knowledge. Spontaneity would apply to the respective realms of practice and knowledge, and the question would arise about the inherent ground in spontaneity which turns it in either direction. Here Kant preserves one of the traditional components of the notion of freedom, that which connotes the situation of being unrestrained by an outside cause, but he superimposes restraint by the spontaneous quality of reason. Since freedom is rooted in reason, the restraint characteristic of the structure of reason which is the faculty of principles, is unavoidable. As far as reason is concerned the origin of freedom necessarily carries guidance with it. But if this is so, to what extent is freedom distinct from reason, or do the two components or phenomena virtually coincide?

Kant tries to evade this difficulty by indicating that the determining ground of freedom's acceptance of the guidance of reason lies in freedom itself. Here he identifies free will with freedom: A will must be conceived as wholly independent of the natural law of appearances; its acceptance of the legislative form of maxims as its sole sufficient determining ground is thus determined by itself.[39] But if this is so, Kant is introducing an aspect of choice or preference into the notion of freedom. Choice and preference are produced by spontaneity as such. The spontaneous will or freedom – and this is actually a tautology – opts for the guidance provided by reason and directly becomes an act preferring what ought to be preferred. Kant is, perhaps unconsciously, at this point close to the Socratic tradition as expressed, for instance by Xenophon who said that to have freedom is to do what is best positing freedom in contrast to the bondage to bodily pleasures. If this is so, then we have to distinguish, as Aristotle did, between voluntary acts and choice; spontaneity has to be qualified, since acts performed on the spur of the moment are described as voluntary, but not as chosen.[40] The choice implied in freedom is detachment from the influence of sensibility to opt for reason. If this is so, then we come back to our previous point namely that

[38] *Ibid.*, p. 75; p. 93.
[39] *Kr.d.p.V.*, p. 33; p. 28.
[40] *Nic. Ethics*, 1111; Ross' transl., p. 53.

the very option for reason is freedom; that option in turn provides for what can be called guided spontaneity as opposed to absolute spontaneity which would be self-generation without a direction. The act implied in freedom would amount to an option. The character of freedom is retained in the act of option, since the rules and maxims of reason are not external forces but built into the very structure and nature of reason. There is no principle external to reason, and both freedom and reason, insofar as they can be distinguished, are within the realm of immanence. This is how Kant is led to identify freedom with the moral law, though the moral law as such is grounded in the reason which guides the choice: "The moral law, however, is a sufficient and original source of determination within us: so it does not for a moment permit us to cast about for a ground of determination external to itself."[41] Kant as a rule presents his point in the following manner: human nature does not of its own proper motion accord with the good. It does so only by virtue of the dominion which reason exercises over sensibility. It is the mind which enables human nature to overcome the hindrance of sensibility by means of moral principles.[42] But there is actually an inter-mediary – mediating between human nature and the good, and that inter-mediary is freedom. After all, it is freedom which is guided by moral princi-ples and thus exposed to the force of the mind, not sensibility in its direct manifestations. To have "free deliberation upon fundamental principles"[43] presupposes "the good offices" of freedom, since sensibility as such cannot deliberate upon fundamental principles. There is therefore a second act implied in Kant, in addition to that previously indicated: an act emancipa-ting us from the bondage to sensibility thus making us free and in addition the supplementary act implied in opting for reason. While the second act can be said to be encompassed by the immanence of spontaneity, the former has to take place somewhere on the borderline between empirical reality and human nature and the level of spontaneity proper. Both acts are acts of choice and option. We choose freedom and we choose the guidance by reason, but there is a sequence of these particular acts.

A similar consideration appears in the attempt to assess the moral quality of acts, or in trying to understand where goodness appears in this context. Insofar as the absolute necessity of the moral order goes, the action is ob-viously looked upon as wholly contingent physically, since there is no physical determination for the moral option. Hence what *ought* necessarily to

[41] *Kr.d.U.*, p. 123; p. 128.
[42] *Ibid.*, p. 119; p. 124.
[43] *Ibid.*

happen frequently does not happen.[44] The goodness of the act lies first in the preference given to the *ought*. The ought in turn is good, or the imperative is identical with the quality insofar as the universalization prescribed by reason is inherent in the ought. By removing ourselves from the contingencies of the physical order and accepting the order of reason, the ought appears imbued with the direction of reason. To put it differently: how can the structure of reason be turned into an imperative when spontaneity is inherent in reason, and when, from the point of view of reason, it does not carry the meaning and the impact of an imperative? To become an imperative presupposes the existence of somebody inspired by the imperative. Only an empirical human being opting for freedom and thus opting for reason can make the rules of reason binding on himself inasmuch as they embody that which ought to happen as an obligation as opposed to that which happens in fact. Kant has to assume the existence of empirical human beings not only as a starting point for the sequence of acts described, but also as an addressee for the spontaneity of reason and the obligations emerging from it. However, the content of the obligation and the obliged – human – subject are by no means identical.

Precisely because we emphasize the acts in Kant's description of practice, in the strictly moral sense, the acts described have but one direction: from the empirical human being up to the spontaneous rules of reason which guide freedom. Yet Kant did not address himself systematically to the question of the transition downwards from the rules of reason to the empirical deeds which occur in the sphere of sensibility and nature. We will come to some of Kant's reflections on empirical human deeds as historical and educational activity later on, in order to elucidate the question of the at-least-*post-factum* systematization of the different levels of human acts and their respective directions.

5

What is the quality of goodness inherent in freedom, which makes it *ab initio* a moral phenomenon or at least an agent of morality? We must of course refrain from committing a naturalistic fallacy in trying to define the moral quality of freedom, but it is nevertheless mandatory to circumscribe it with some precision. This will be done with full awareness of the fact that Kant himself did not explicate the identification of practice and morality, or

---

[44] *Ibid.*, p. 269; vol. II, p. 58.

that of freedom and morality. It goes without saying that the usual descriptions and contradistinctions suggested by Kant, like the contradistinction between the physical good and the moral good or between virtue and the easy life "*Wohlleben*," are not very helpful in an attempt to discern the particular character of moral good.

A distinction between three components in Kant's moral evaluation of freedom will be suggested, although the convergence between these three components is open to question.

(*a*) The first aspect of goodness inherent in freedom is that of freedom as activating a potentiality, as empirical man's potential to become a free or intelligible agent, or to make himself an intelligible cause. The empirical human being or subject together with all causality in the field of appearance contains certain conditions in terms of noumenon. These must be regarded as purely intelligible. The intelligible ground does not have to be considered in empirical enquiries, since it only concerns thought in the pure understanding even though the effects of the thought and the activity of pure understanding are to be met with in the field of appearances. Yet, in spite of the determination by the intelligible cause, these appearances must be capable of complete causal explanation in terms of other appearances in accordance with natural laws. Man, who knows all the rest of nature solely through his senses, knows himself through pure apperception. His knowledge is acquired in acts of inner determination which cannot be regarded as impressions of the senses.[45]

The duality so sharply presented by Kant does not have to be dwelt upon here. This context requires that we concern ourselves with the coexistence of the two lines of causality and with the fact that Kant specifically refers to man in both causal contexts. Man is capable of being determined by intelligible causality, and he is an intelligible cause. The manifestation and explication of this causality is to be found in the moral sphere, i.e. in the formulation of the "ought." This indeed is a paradoxical kind of potentiality: evidently there is no line of continuity from the empirical causal series to intelligible causality, but the latter is nevertheless within the will. It therefore seems good to explicate man's potential for initiating intelligible causality, for, without this explication and activation the human potentiality would not reach its fulfillment. Between empirical man and intelligible character there is indeed a leap, but it does not lead to a divine sphere; the agent remains within that of broad human potentialities. Kant would not say, of course, that freedom is a *telos* of empirical man in the sense that it represents his continuous

---

[45] *Kr.d.r.V.*, p. 573–575; p. 471–472.

actualization. But he still implies that freedom is a *telos* of empirical man in spite of all the concessions he makes to the fact that there is no direct line of transition from empirical data to the level of the intelligible character. Kant retains the rhythm of potentiality and actualization without subscribing to the elements of Aristotelian metaphysics.

(*b*) The second component of freedom is that from which freedom gains its particular moral quality. While the first component relates to actualization, the second relates to the act of opting for the universality of the moral law and its application to all human beings, granting that they are an end. The second component of the phenomenon of freedom in a combination of several elements: there is a quality of being good in the very act or attitude of opting – and in this sense the second component is a continuation of the first, since opting would not be possible on the level of empirical causality. But this is not enough: goodness here goes together with granting, with openness, with being forthcoming. In this sense goodness is essentially anti-egoistic, since it is guided by the universal rule or is itself the universal rule of regarding all human beings equally as an end. What is given or granted here, and this indeed is the quality of goodness, is a new perspective vis-à-vis human beings. This perspective, by definition, removes human beings from their involvement in the world of appearances and puts them on the level of ends, which have no systematic place in the sphere of appearances. Freedom belongs to morality as a *conditio sine qua non* for an option separating the agent from its determination by natural laws and because its absorption of the universal law opens a new vista for human attitudes and for the sake of enduring human character. The characteristic feature of Kant's theory of ethics is probably to be found in this context. Morality is related to a new outlook, more than to concrete human deeds. This shift in emphasis is a consequence of the point made previously, that deeds cannot be removed from the empirical sphere and thus from their subjection to natural laws of causality. It is one of the most characteristic marks of Kant's ethical philosophy that morality is bound up with perspectives and attitudes more than with concrete actions and acts. This shift enables Kant to come to grips with many empirical problems, including problems of history and, as we shall see presently, the problem of evil.

(*c*) Here again, the distinction between freedom as an option and spontaneity as a characteristic of reason must be reformulated. Spontaneity can be understood negatively as lack of determination by an outside factor, or as a self-sufficient activity. It is in this sense we can say that for Kant spontaneity as moral goodness amounts to self-sufficiency. Kant comes back here to some of the classical interpretations both of freedom and autarcheia. As

Aristotle said, in *Metaphysics* 982b, a free man lives his life for his own sake and not for that of others. Aristotle adds that philosophy is free in the same way, for it alone exists for its own sake. This notion of freedom as self-sufficiency clearly led Aristotle in his analysis of the first cause as an unmoved mover. Proklos, in a way, continued this line of reasoning when he analysed that which proceeds from what he called another cause. Such an entity is subordinate to principles which derive their substance from themselves, but these principles in turn have what he called a self-constituted existence. Proklos continues his reasoning as follows: "If there be nothing self-consti-tutive, there will be no true self-sufficiency in anything. [The self-sufficient] has more likeness to the good itself (yet falls short, in that it participates good and is not itself the primal good), it is in some way akin to the good, inasmuch as it can furnish its good out of its own being . . ."[46] Kant's ethical theory in its relation to the ultimate datum of the spontaneity of reason can be interpreted as a theory which ultimately identifies the self-sufficiency in-herent in spontaneity with the good. Now, although spontaneity makes freedom possible, it is not only, as we have seen, an operative quality. It is an ultimate datum; it relates not only to the moral direction but also to the theoretical sphere. The moral direction is only one manifestation of sponta-neity, as such supported by the two components discerned above. Since Kant puts self-sufficiency on the level of spontaneity, we can conclude by saying that self-sufficiency is realized on the level of reason and that its realization does not require a shift from reason to the divine essence.

Having analysed the three components of Kant's ethical theory, it is necessary to add a word of caution to preclude the myopic conclusion, that there is full harmony between the three components. There is not: with regard to the first and the third components, there is a difference between potentiality and full actuality, since spontaneity as self-sufficiency is a kind of full actuality on the level of reason, but not on the level of the world. Moreover, there is a difference between the second and the third component, since the second component contains both a factor of being an agent and a factor of the universality of the sphere of deeds as an open sphere; that very openness provides for the moral quality of universality. In the third component on the other hand there is no openness, since self-sufficiency is self-enclosed in one of its aspects. Obviously the more Kant removes ethical theory from the sphere of openness to the sphere of mere spontaneity, en-

---

[46] See: Proklus *The Elements of Theology*, revised text with translation, introduction and commentary by E.R. Dodds, Oxford, at the Clarendon Press, 1964, proposition 40, p. 43; proposition 9, p. 11.

closed in itself as it is, he *pari passu* removes himself from the locus of human deeds in their historical and to his mind sensuous manifestations.[47]

6

This may be summarized by a paraphrase of one of the most renowned metaphors of Greek philosophy. Kant's theory of practice amounts to turning the will towards the moral law and to the assumption of a kinship between the will and the moral law, which makes this "turning" possible. This is parallel to Plato turning the eyes of the soul to ideas: here the soul belongs to the world of ideas, and so the turning is not an imposition but an act of recollection. The question for Kant is: how does the will come back down to the cave? As we shall see, although it is possibly an attempt to resolve this dilemma, Kant's theory of evil does not do so. We now turn to a few comments on his theory of evil.

Freedom of the will as an initiating factor to action is exhibited in the fact that it operates only insofar as the individual has incorporated it into his maxim. Only in this sense does the general rule in accordance with which man conducts himself coexist with the absolute spontaneity of the will.[48] The distinction between a good man and an evil man cannot lie in the difference between the incentives they adopt into their maxim or in the content of the maxim. The difference depends rather upon which maxim is made subordinate to or conditional for the other. It is man's free decision to make his sensuous nature the incentive he adopts into his maxim in accordance with the principle of self-love. Hence the evil man is evil only in reversing the moral order of the incentives.[49] Self-love means total opposition to universalization and universality in the sense discussed above, since self-love does not leave the agent open to viewing other human beings as ends,

---

[47] The interrelation between freedom and the moral law is stated by Kant himself: freedom is 'certainly the *ratio essendi* of the moral law, the latter is the *ratio cognoscendi* of freedom.' Kant elaborates this circularity by saying: "For had not the moral law already been distinctly thought in our reason, we would never have been justified in assuming anything like freedom ... But if there were no freedom, the moral law would never have been encountered in us.' (*Kr.d.p.V.*, p. 4 note). Kant clearly indicates the circular interaction between freedom and the moral law. He does not assume their identity. This is indeed an illuminating comment on the structure of Kant's system, but, as we shall see, it is doubtful whether it is an exhaustive exposition. See the present author's: Desire and Spontaneity, *The Review of Metaphysics*, Vol. XXX, No. September 1976, p. 38ff.

[48] *Religion*, p. 19.

[49] *Ibid.*, p. 31.

but only makes him capable of viewing himself as an end. The evil man is a man, to paraphrase a Hebrew saying, who knows the good and rebels against it. He deliberately opts not for universality but for self-love and the sensuality motivating it. The evil man is posited within the framework of the distinction between the empirical and intelligible character: he is a man who is already on the level of the intelligible character but does not proceed to the substantive supplement of intelligibility, that is to say, to the moral law in its universal meaning and application, let alone to the self-sufficiency of reason which clearly contradicts the self-referential or egotistic character of self-love. Kant's analysis of evil is significant not only in its own right but also because of the fact that it sheds light on some of the distinct problems of the phenomenology of freedom. The evil man is a free man who does not activate his freedom in the prescribed direction; he is not using his freedom as a unification of choice and the prescribed rule or in the direction of that unification. The evil man separates, as it were, the operative ingredient inherent in freedom from its prescribed combination with the "ought." The evil man realizes his freedom by following the 'is" and not by opting for the "ought." We can thus conclude that Kant did not assume a pre-established harmony between freedom and its proper direction. He viewed the separation of freedom from the rule as potentially evil. Freedom's choice of sensuality is an evil act. The line leading upwards in the three components of freedom is that from potentiality to self-sufficiency; the line leading down into the 'cave," i.e. evil is ultimately the choice for the empirical motivating forces of human nature and behaviour. The evil man prefers the empirical when he should prefer the intelligible. The intelligible stimulating factor leads man to revert to his empirical existence and adopt it. But this is where Kant could not find a harmonious solution for the two lines of his own analysis, that leading from the empirical to the intelligible, and that leading from the intelligible to the empirical. The first is directed towards the good, the second directed towards evil. This is why Kant tried, in his various historical reflections, if not to remove evil, at least to incorporate it in the broader sphere of acts and events leading to the realization of the good in spite of themselves as part of his doctrine. This is dealt with at length. But before embarking on that analysis, it is necessary to pay some attention to the notion of the primacy of practical reason.

7

Primacy can be understood in several ways. Let us begin with what might be called its technical connotation. Kant describes this aspect of primacy as a prerogative (*Vorzug*) of what he calls the practical interest insofar as different interests are subordinated to it and the particular interest is not inferior to any other. To be sure, reason underlies all interests or, more specifically, practical as well as theoretical interest. Reason determines the interest of all powers of the mind. There is a speculative or theoretical interest which consists of the knowledge of objects, and a practical interest which consists of the determination of the will with respect to the final and perfect end. Should different interests conflict, like the theoretical interest directed towards an object and the practical interest directed to an end, the question arises as to which interest is superior. This is why Kant tries to delineate the technical meaning of the primacy of practical interest which is grounded in practical reason, inasmuch as some notions which are beyond the scope of cognitive and theoretical powers of the mind are essential for the full development of practical interest and for the activation of practical reason. Kant moves from a general delineation of the superiority of practical reason to the notion of the postulates of pure practical reason – i.e. the immortality of the soul, the existence of God. This portion of Kant's doctrine is well-known.[50] But it needs to be reiterated, precisely because practical interest tips the scales, that the same reason judges *a priori* by principles whether the judgment is expressed for theoretical or for practical purposes. Since the same reason operates in both cases, the primacy established exists within the same scope. Should the capacity of theoretical reason not suffice to establish propositions positively, and should these propositions in turn not contradict the theoretical interest, reason must assume that, once they are sufficiently verified (*beglaubigt*), these propositions belong to the practical interest of pure reason. Yet Kant emphasizes on the one hand that the common ground is reason, and on the other the fact that the pursuit of practical interest does not grow out of pure reason but comes from without.[51] This is not quite consistent, because, after all, both the cognitive and the practical interest are grounded in reason and the option for the practical interest does not therefore emerge from an extraneous factor outside or beyond reason. The most that can be said is that although it emerges from reason the practical interest does not emerge directly from theoretical interest, in spite of the fact that the theoretical pursuit of reason deals with concepts like immortality of the soul and God, without being able to provide theoretical grounds for the validity and assessment of their place. Be that as it may, the technical meaning of primacy can be summarized by saying that

[50] *Kr.d.p.V.*, p. 138; p. 124.
[51] *Ibid.*, p. 139; p. 125–126.

primacy amounts to attributing superiority to one realm of interest vis-à-vis another.

The broader connotation of primacy does not relate to primacy validating an option in the event that two interests conflict, but has to do with the primacy of the sphere to which the interest refers. There is a primacy of the practical, because the sphere of practice is superior in the broad scope of systematic philosophy which is philosophy of reason, or philosophy of spontaneity. It is in this sense that we have to interpret the renowned statement: "I have therefore found it necessary to deny *knowledge* in order to make room for faith,"[52] and the parallel statement, although it is not so very radical: "For although we have to surrender the language of *knowledge*, we still have sufficient ground to employ, in the presence of the most exacting reason, the quite legitimate language of a firm faith."[53] The sharpness of Kant's expressions and even the precise meaning of the term faith may be disregarded here, except for noting that faith connotes the expectation of a total and harmonious moral order. What Kant was really seeking was to ascertain the systematic place of morals and of what he called the metaphysics of morals. The systematic superiority or primacy of morality lies in the fact that "... morality is the only code of laws applying to our actions which can be derived completely *a priori* from principles."[54] This is because the concern with essential ends is a concern with nothing less than man's whole destiny and the philosophy dealing with this destiny is called moral philosophy. "On account of this superiority which moral philosophy has over all other occupations of reason"[55] – moral philosophy is given superiority because its subject matter is man's ends or destiny. The intelligible world (*mundus intelligibilis*) is in truth the moral world (*mundus moralis*). Primacy or superiority is grounded in the superior place of the intelligible sphere and in its identification with the moral sphere. This identification is due to the factors analysed previously: the sphere of morality is the sphere of pure reason: it is not based upon reason's concretization in sensible data, but upon legislation by reason; and its structure is not that of the subsumption characteristic of a cognitive sphere, but that of obedience. The moral sphere as an intelligible sphere creates its own field of realization, that of freedom, and conversely, does not need support beyond its own legislation. It even rejects such support; evil *a limine*, as we have seen, is not grounded in an *urge*, but in an *option* for sensuality. Insofar as Kant uses

[52] *Kr.d.r.V.*, p. XXX; p. 29.
[53] *Ibid.*, p. 773; p. 597.
[54] *Ibid.*, p. 869; p. 659.
[55] *Ibid.*, p. 868; p. 658.

the term *mundus intelligibilis,* he is objectively placing his terminology as
well as his doctrine in the tradition which made the Latin term the equivalent
of the Greek term *cosmos noëtós.* This connoted the sum total of ideas in
the Platonic sense, or the sum total of ideal objects insofar as they coincided
with what is objectively intellectual or spiritual. Kant tried to safeguard
objectivity and ideality in immanence. Spontaneous reason is the ultimate
datum. It prescribes objective, universally binding laws; spontaneous reason
with all its immanence, is therefore the locus of objectivity. It is because of
this combination of spontaneity, objectivity, intelligibility and morality that
Kant came to assume the architectonic or systematic primacy of practice
as morality, rather than its primacy only in a conflict of different pursuits.

There is an additional consideration which probably explains the primacy
of practice *qua* morality, and this is related to Kant's concept of the realm
(*Reich*): "We are indeed legislative members of a moral realm which is
possible through freedom and which is presented to us as an object of respect
by practical reason; yet we are at the same time subjects in it, not sovereigns
... ."[56] The very fact that Kant uses the term realm is characteristic of the
direction of his teaching, since the same term is employed for the divine
realm,[57] which is coterminous with the reality of the supreme good, or with
a totally intelligible world.[58] The moral human being creates a realm analo-
gous to the realm of God, and is endowed with a productive capacity. This
capacity is in turn another ground for the supremacy of the practical and
moral, since the moral realm is an embodiment of human creativity which
is related to the notion of *imago dei.* It is clear that in this broad sense, the
supremacy of the practical transcends the technicalities of clashes in a
particular philosophical presentation dealing with such concepts as the
immortality of the soul or even the existence of God. The broad notion of
primacy leads to the structuring of meaningful spheres, as in the case of the
relation between cognition of data and self-legislation. Kant refers to phili-
sophy as wisdom (*Weisheit*) in this latter sense. Wisdom is a practical idea;
it is the idea of the lawfully-perfect, practical use of reason.[59] The distinction
has to be maintained not only between different expressions of philosophy,
but between science critically pursued and methodically directed, and the
doctrine of wisdom. Science is only a narrow gateway leading to wisdom,
not merely in the sense of what one ought to do, but in the sense of what
should guide teachers in laying down the path to wisdom which everyone

---

[56] *Kr.d.p.V.,* p. 96; p. 85.
[57] *Ibid.,* p. 83; p. 73.
[58] *Ibid.,* p. 157; p. 142.
[59] *Anthropologie,* p. 101.

should follow and in keeping others from going astray.[60] But wisdom as the epitomy of the supremacy of moral and practical concerns creates some serious problems, when we pursue Kant's last statement about the extent to which practice percolates down to the level of action, or ceases to be an interplay between law and freedom and becomes integrated in acts. We shall now see that some of Kant's presentations in line with his systematic architectonics show that Kant himself hesitated on this rather sensitive point. This will be the next part of our analysis.

8

Let us introduce into the context of our analysis the notion "canon." Kant understood "canon" in accordance with medieval legal terminology, as "the sum total of the *a priori* principles of the correct employment of certain faculties of knowledge." As an obvious example for the canon, the general logic is referred to, since it is a canon for the form of understanding and reason. There is also a canon of the pure understanding which consists of *a priori* modes of knowledge. But the applicability of the canon is confined to the correct employment of a faculty of knowledge. There is therefore no canon for the speculative uses of pure reason. A canon for pure reason is possible only for its practical employment.[61] But what does the practical employment of reason mean? Kant is obviously concerned with practice *qua* morality here, thus once again delineating the broad contours of morality. But since we are considering a canon, we have to be more specific about the rules for its employment, and even about its sphere of employment. Does Kant say no more about reason and its canon than that reason is an incentive for freedom, or does he go beyond the conjunction analysed previously of the option and the rule? After all, the practical aspect of reason, the rules and structure formulated in the canon for its employment, do not indicate performance or execution of an imperative. At most they indicate that one is engaged in obeying a rule, and perhaps not only intellectually, that is to say, that one is being shaped by the rule. The moral law has its effect or *must* have its effect on the mind.[62] Practice as engaged in respect (*Achtung*), respect being a feeling produced by an intellectual cause (*Grund*),[63] but not an accomplishment like the production of certain ends. Respect for the

---

[60] *Kr.d.p.V.*, p. 188; p. 168.
[61] *Kr.d.v.V.*, p. 824–825; p. 629–630.
[62] *Kr.d.p.V.*, p. 85; p. 75.
[63] *Ibid.*, p. 86; p. 76.

moral law amounts to the reciprocity between human beings, expressed in the mutual recognition of human beings as ends. But all this is still a long way from action. We are still within the orbit of *actio immanens;* and this employment occurs within the limits of that self-enclosed orbit.

A juxtaposition of cognitive understanding, *Verstand*, and practical reason leads to even more radical results. Cognitive understanding is open to data essentially because it is void unless data are provided. It applies to data through intermediaries like *a priori* forms of sensibility as well as schemata. Practical reason *qua* pure reason is self-contained. It is not void because it contains the *a priori* conjunction of freedom and law and the interplay between the two. It is by definition imbued with rules of employment and although the rules, allegedly contained under the heading of the canon, do not exist, they are virtually not needed. Hence Kant's problem is bound to be that of employing his ethical structure for actions performed, accomplished or executed. Kant says that practical reason does not require schemata, but the question is whether this is merely a privilege or whether it is really – and also – a problem. Kant has to appeal to practical judgment (*praktische Urteilskraft*) to decide whether an action which is possible in the world of sensibility is a case under the rule. It is practical judgment which applies what the rule asserts universally or *in abstracto* to an action *in concreto*.[64]

But the question is not confined to the transition from abstractness to concreteness; it also relates to the transition from concreteness to abstractness, or in other words to the problem of whether an act or performance taking place in the empirical realm has a moral meaning, the problem of whether it has been motivated by the moral law and obedience to it. To rely on judgment or *Urteilskraft* is perhaps more precarious in the moral field than in any other. The perplexity of the *Urteilskraft* results from the rather subtle distinctions between the pragmatic and the practical. *Urteilskraft* (*judicium*), which cannot be taught but only exercised, is that capacity whose direction is that what is opportune, what is done, and what is proper (*tunlich, sich schickt, sich geziemt*).[65] Because this is the price practical reason pays for its purity, Kant has to attempt to establish links between the sphere of purity and the sphere of sensibility, precisely insofar as historical human acts are concerned. Anticipating one of our conclusions we may say that these links at most indicate *post factum* affinities between deeds occurring in time and practical reason as pure reason. This is the only systematic possibility open to Kant: since pure reason does not go beyond its defined

---

[64] *Ibid.*, p. 79; p. 70.
[65] *Anthropologie*, p. 99.

scope, while the sphere of sensibility is an empirical reality, the two can only meet in fact, and there is no *a priori* ground for their convergence.

9

The difference between Kant's emphasis on practical reason, or on the combination of reason and practice, and freedom as choice, in Aristotle's position on these issues requires a comment. This difference cannot be obliterated by the fact that Aristotle uses the notion of the architectonic form of practical wisdom, which is what he called legislated wisdom, *nomothetiké*.[66] Kant uses the term legislation of human reason too, but in Kant it is the essence of philosophy which has two objects, nature and freedom. Philosophy therefore contains not only the law of nature but also the moral law. It presents them as two distinct systems at first, although they are ultimately embraced in one philosophical system.[67] The employment of the same term "legislative" *nomothetiké* should not lead us astray. First of all Kant transposes reason's legislative capacity to the philosophy of nature too or, conversely, does not confine it to practice. Secondly, whereas Aristotle confines legislative wisdom to practical wisdom, and is therefore concerned with human happiness and not the moral law as an end, – for Kant it is obviously the latter which is the end. Here is the difference between Aristotle's notion of the practical thinking or practical wisdom, and Kant's notion of theory and practice or practical reason: for Aristotle theory is concerned with the necessary or with the invariable; for Kant theory – or knowledge – is concerned with variables which it unifies by necessary principles which do not derive their necessity from the variables but impose it on them. Theory is *pari passu* concerned with the contingent or variable, whereas for Kant it is practice which is concerned with the necessary or invariable, albeit in Kant's special sense. For Aristotle practical wisdom is applied to the appetitive and to the desiring element in the soul, whereas for Kant the appetitive and the desiring are *ab initio* beyond the scope of his ethical system. Hence for Kant practical reason guides the option for the law and adopts the chosen guidance, whereas for Aristotle the practical intellect aims at truth in agreement with right desire.[68] We can make this point clearer by saying that for Kant there is no right desire, since reverence or respect is the only adequate attitude towards the moral law. Moreover,

---

[66] *Nic. Eth.*, 1141; Ross' transl., p. 147.
[67] *Kr.d.r.V.*, p. 868; p. 658–659.
[68] *Nic. Eth.*, 1139; Ross' transl., p. 139.

practical wisdom makes us adopt the right means.[69] Aristotle concludes by pointing what is evident, namely that it is impossible to be practically wise without being good,[70] while for Kant to be practically wise in his sense, that is to say, to be motivated by pure reason, is *eo ipso* to be good.

This leads us to our second comparison, that between Aristotle's notion of choice or *prohaíresis* and Kant's notion of will or freedom. Aristotle says[71] that choice is the efficient cause but not the final cause in which action originates. Choice is desire and reasoning with a view to an end. For Kant on the other hand choice *qua* freedom is both the efficient cause of action and its final cause, since, if action has an end, it is to perpetuate freedom; freedom is both and intelligible cause and the intelligible receptacle for the intelligible law. Choice is for Kant obviously not a combination of desire and reasoning with a view to an end, because freedom as choice is an end in itself and because it is initiated by reason or identical with it. It is obviously not a desire, either in the Aristotelian or in the Kantian sense. For Aristotle man is the *arché* or moving principle of his actions.[72] Since choice begets action, Aristotle describes *prohaíresis* as taking place for the sake of something. *Prohaíresis* is related to deliberation, and we deliberate, as Aristotle says, not about ends but about means;[73] his examples are deliberately trivial, for instance, whether this is bread or whether it has been baked as it should. The end cannot be a subject of deliberation. If we were to be always deliberating, we would have to go on doing so to infinity. Whenever an agent chooses the means to an end after deliberation, his action is voluntary and takes place by choice.[74]

Here is Aristotle's formulation of man as the *arché* or begetter of his actions: "For every one ceases to enquire how he is to act when he has brought the moving principle back to himself and to the ruling part of himself; for this is what chooses."[75] Taking this as the motto for our concluding comparison between Kant and Aristotle, we can say that Aristotle presents choice as an "anthropocentric" phenomenon, while Kant presents it, if we include will and freedom in choice, as a "ratiocentric" phenomenon. Aristotle considers choice grounded in the agent an ultimate decision and an ultimate explanation of the action; Kant considers the motivation by the moral law grounded in reason the ultimate anchor of the action or the choice

[69] *Nic. Eth.*, 1144; Ross' transl., p. 155.
[70] *Nic. Eth.*, 1144; Ross' transl., p. 156.
[71] *Nic. Eth.*, 1139; Ross' transl., p. 139.
[72] *Nic. Eth.*, 1113; Ross' transl., p. 59.
[73] *Nic. Eth.*, 1112; Ross' transl., p. 57.
[74] *Nic. Eth.*, 1113; Ross' transl., p. 61.
[75] *Nic. Eth.*, 1113; Ross' transl., p. 57–58.

expressed in action. Though both Aristotle and Kant speak of choice and of the combination of practice and wisdom, it is clear that Aristotle is concerned with the situation and with the deliberation guiding the choice, whereas Kant is concerned with the law. The law is universal by definition and can only be grounded in the faculty of universal principles, namely in reason. The shift from the situation to reason is reinforced by the fact that Kant superimposed the notion of sublimity on the sphere of morality. This aspect of Kant's theory will now be analysed adding a comment on Aristotle first.

This description of practical wisdom calls for a qualification with reference to what Aristotle says about virtue as a mean; it is necessary to distinguish clearly within the range of the English terminology between a *mean* and a *means*. Aristotle says of the mean that it is determined by a rational principle "and by that principle by which the man of practical wisdom would determine it."[76] Practical wisdom here determines the proper course of action as the right mean between two extremes. In this context, practical wisdom obviously does not guide man as to how he is to apply the means to an end. It shapes the proper course between guiding passions which on their own would be excessive. Only wisdom keeps the balance, and in this sense wisdom always applies to passions and not to a guiding principle in the sense in which Kant uses the term. Granting this qualification, we can conclude by saying that Aristotle takes wisdom not as corresponding to a principle but as the mediating link between the principle and the actions and passions which are the starting point for the problem of applying wisdom.

The term sublimity, as it appears in Kant, is clearly a variation on the classical Greek concept of *hýpsos*. It is well known that traditionally the concept had both an aesthetic and an ethical connotation. Kant preserves the two connotations although probably he would prefer to give even the aesthetic aspect an ethical meaning. The terms beauty (*Schönheit*) and sublimity (*Erhabenheit*), Kant gave in the various phases of his philosophical development different meanings. Thus, for instance, he said on one occasion that sublimity moves, beauty stimulates (*Erhabenheit rührt, Schönheit reizt*).[77] Elsewhere he distinguishes between being favourably disposed (*Wohlgewogenheit*) and respect (*Achtung*); the first refers to beauty, the latter to sublimity. But from the point of view of Kant's notion of practice, the introduction of the term respect or reverence for sublimity reinforces the point made in our previous analysis: "This idea of personality awakens respect;

[76] *Nic. Eth.*, 1000; Ross' transl., p. 39.
[77] Consult: W.F.R. Hardie, *Aristotle's Ethical Theory*, Oxford, at the Clarendon Press, 1968, pp. 212ff., 160ff.

it places before our eyes the sublimity of our own nature (in its [higher] vocation), while it shows us at the same time the unsuitability of our conduct to it, thus striking down our self-conceit."[78] This statement clearly refers to human nature not as given datum but as a vocation, though it implies the eventual identification of this vocation with the moral law or with obedience to it grounded in freedom. The transition described previously from empirical nature to what might here be called intelligible nature, (although this may sound like a *contradictio in adjecto*) again comes into prominence. Empirical nature is denigrated precisely because of the awareness of intelligible nature and its identification with vocation or moral fulfillment. But in a different context Kant applies the adjective "sublime" to actions performed with great sacrifice merely for the sake of duty which can be praised as noble and sublime deeds.[79] Kant is apparently trying to find a link between the extra-moral position of empirical human nature and the moral status of the vocation of human nature: "It is a very sublime thing in human nature to be determined to actions directly by a pure law of reason, and even the illusion wherein the subjective element of this intellectual determination of the will is held to be sensuous and an effect of a particular sensuous feeling ... partakes of this sublimity."[80] It is clear that Kant is here combining human nature and the law of pure reason as determining action. The very fact that human nature is capable of elevating itself to the level of the moral law and its incentive renders human nature sublime. It is clear that Kant hesitates between a view which disregards empirical human nature and another view which elevates it. He then seeks a *locus standi* for the moral law and presents empirical human nature as lying in between: inasmuch as it is empirical, it cannot have a moral position and is before or outside practice. But as potentially determined by the moral law, human nature loses its empirical frame and gains a moral position.

Referring to the qualified parallels between nature in the metaphysics of nature and in the metaphysics of morals, Kant says that the metaphysics of nature explore the principles for the application of nature's universal highest presupposition to objects of experience. Similarly, the metaphysics of morals cannot be unconcerned about man's particular nature. This is known only through experience, and it must be made an object for analysis in order to show that consequences (*Folgerungen*) derived from universal moral principles. The reference to experience does not impair the purity of moral principles, nor does its origin thereby become doubtful *a priori*. After this description

---

[78] *Kr.d.p.V.*, p. 102; p. 90.
[79] *Ibid.*, p. 99; p. 88.
[80] *Ibid.*, p. 135; p. 121.

of the parallelism between the two aspects of metaphysics, the following statement is made: "This means as much as: a metaphysic of morals cannot be grounded in anthropology, but still can be applied to it."[81] The relationship between anthropology and moral philosophy is, as we see, a one-way relationship. Moral philosophy is not based upon anthropology, which is to say that moral laws cannot be derived from human nature. An even more forcible formulation would be that such a derivation would amount to a self-contradiction. But the concern with human nature is directed by moral philosophy and human nature as analysed in anthropology, contains features cognate to the moral level or at least capable of a moral transformation, even if this transformation will be radical. One of the expressions of this ultimately positive relationship between human nature and the moral vocation is to call human nature sublime. The human potential is imbued with a sublimity which emanates from the sublime actuality of the moral law. Still as we have seen, sublimity is not only attributed to empirical human nature but also to particular acts which are grounded in the moral law. Here Kant did not raise the question of the transition from the moral law to empirical human nature and to the empirical human being who performs acts characterized by nobility and sublimity. Kant's programmatic assumption that there is a way down from moral philosophy to anthropology raises the question of the scope of anthropology – and many ambiguities remain in the Kantian system on this central issue.[82]

When we move on to a detailed analysis of Kant's concept of happiness, we will see that Kant struggles there too with the question of empirical human aspirations and their position in the moral sphere.[83]

[81] *Met.d.S.*, p. 15–16.
[82] On the notion of sublimity consult the present author's: Sublimity and Terror, in *Idealistic Studies, An International Philosophical Journal*, vol. III, No. 3, Sept. 1973, p. 238ff.
A central theme of Kant's moral philosophy is analysed in the present author's forthcoming book *Man and His Dignity*.
[83] On the polemics centered round the pure character of the moral imperative consult: Eberhard Günter Schulz, *Rehbergs Opposition Gegen Kants Ethik*, Köln, Wien, Böhlau Verlag, 1975.

CHAPTER TWO

WORTHINESS AND REWARD

1

The question now centers on the reasons Kant does not put the idea of happiness within the sphere of ethics proper. He still retains its relationship to ethics but at the same time transcends it or withdraws from it. Our assumption is that the concept of happiness is far from unambiguous and that it is interpreted differently in different philosophical systems. The place of happiness in Kant's system is related to the particular meaning he gives that concept. We begin with an exposition of some of the meanings of the concept of happiness.

In its basic meaning, the concept may connote a chance, something which comes our way as a result of good fortune; it is thus a situation that is fortuitous. A different connotation is that which relates happiness to the achievement of a goal or situation considered to be good. Unlike the first meaning of happiness where the situation is simply there as a result of a haphazard coincidence, this meaning indicates an attainment. It can be viewed as a deliberate attainment accompanied by the recognition that the situation attained has been our goal from the very beginning, or as a state of affairs which rightly elicits our consent *post factum*. In this sense we speak of happiness as our state of contentment. The Biblical term "*osher*," as in the Book of Psalms 72, 17, where it is said that all the nation will consent to you (*ye'ashruha*), means to acknowledge, to assent to, and it has also the nuance of to congratulate or call him blessed. The situation of assenting on the one hand, and of being in a position eliciting assent on the other, is sometimes rendered as being blessed or beatified. This appears again in the Biblical phrase "*ashrei ha'ish*" – blessed be the person who assents to a state of affairs in which he finds himself not fortuitously, but as the result of an achievement and through the response of the divine being.

The question confronting us here is why happiness should be placed in the moral realm or why it should be a topic for a theory of morality. To put it differently: what makes happiness a concept which can be regarded as a principle of moral behaviour, or as an objective for moral striving? It stands to reason that happiness is considered a good in terms of consenting to an objective or to a goal. A human being who attains the goal is identified with the state of affairs which rightly elicits in him the awareness that he is happy or that he has achieved happiness. The starting point is an attempt to achieve a goal, and the achieved goal as a final position is supposed to bring about happiness. In this sense, and this takes us a step further, happiness is a situation in which man has reached or created a state of affairs in which his expectations and aspirations are fulfilled. Happiness is thus related to a state of affairs which has a certain finality.

This indicates a situation of harmony between man and his aspirations on the one hand and circumstances of reality on the other. From the moral point of view, happiness can thus be seen in two parallel ways. Happiness indicates a state of affairs where harmony prevails and harmony is considered a goal or a good in itself. Moreover, when harmony is established and not given in the first place, it is a remedy for a situation which lacked harmony, and thus lacked goodness. In this context, happiness is a particular interpretation of the ideal of harmony. Once again, two vistas open up here: either the fundamental objective is to achieve or restore harmony, or it is to attain happiness, the establishment of harmony being the precondition for its attainment.

To view harmony in terms of happiness already gives prominence to the relationship between harmony and human expectations: man finds a response to his aspirations in the situation of harmony. When man recognizes the presence of this response, his recognition leads him to assent to the situation or to affirm it as one which fulfils his aspirations. It is in this sense that we speak of satisfaction, pleasure, contentment, etc. as happiness. This is what is meant by felicity, whereby emphasis is placed on man's relation to the circumstances and not on the objective structure of the circumstances themselves. In any case, harmony is present in both renderings of the concept of happiness. The first rendering relates to harmony in the state of affairs, while the second relates to the harmony between man and the state of affairs. It is in this context that philosophers have suggested different levels of pleasure or satisfaction, and a distinction between a fleeting pleasure and enduring pleasure. When it is understood merely as something which comes our way fortuitously, happiness connotes a transient pleasure, whereas happiness associated with harmony may connote a permanent state of satisfaction.

2

The distinction between different levels of pleasure was formulated by Plato. Plato's presentation is the cornerstone for all the variations on the theme of pleasure to be found in philosophical discourse: "... when we see someone indulging in pleasures, perhaps in the greatest of pleasures, the ridiculous, or disgraceful nature of the action makes us ashamed; and so we put them out of sight, and consign them to darkness, under the idea that they ought not to meet the eye of day." Socrates' reply is that his companion will proclaim everywhere "... that pleasure is not the first of possessions, nor yet the second, but that in measure, and the mean, and the suitable, and the light, the eternal nature has been found." Following this statement Socrates enumerates classes of pleasure: "In the second class is contained the symmetrical and beautiful and perfect or sufficient, and all which are of that family." He places "... mind and wisdom" in the third class, and in the fourth class, "... the goods which we were affirming to appertain specially to the soul – sciences, and arts and true opinions as we called them. These come after the third class, and form the fourth, and they are certainly more akin to good than pleasure is." Then Socrates mentions: "The fifth class are the pleasures which were defined by us as painless, being the pure pleasure or the soul herself, as we turn then, which accompany, some the sciences and some the senses."[1]

What is important in Plato's presentation is that he distinguishes between different sorts of pleasure and orders them in a scale. The proximity between pleasure and the good provides the criterion of order: the good appertains to activities like sciences and arts and to opinions related to truths. Plato laid the foundation for the evaluation of pleasure in the context of human aspirations and in that of certain to-be-defined goals of human activity. In spite of Aristotle's criticism of Plato, it can already be said that Aristotle follows Plato when he refers to different levels of pleasure.

When Aristotle objected to Plato's theory of the state and its ruling class, he argued that Plato deprives the guardians of the state even of happiness, since Plato maintains that happiness pertains to the whole of the state and not to its individual members. Aristotle presents an opposite view, holding that the state as a whole cannot be happy unless most of its parts, or at least some of them, are happy. The quality of being happy is not of the same

---

[1] Philebus, 66, in *The Dialogues of Plato*, translated into English by B. Jowett, with introduction by Prof. Raphael Demos, Vol. II, Random House, New York, 1927, p. 401–402.

order as the quality of being even.[2] Hence the whole cannot be considered happy without reference to its parts. In this context, Aristotle seems to be taking happiness in its broad, or colloquial, sense of pleasure or satisfaction.

Aristotle goes further when he attempts to give happiness a positive status in his theory. He agrees with Plato that happiness is proportionate to the goodness and wisdom of the person enjoying happiness. With regard to the function and destiny of the state, Aristotle maintains that members of the state are entitled to share in its possessions in a ratio which befits them. Leisure is presented either as happiness or as a precondition for pleasure, satisfaction and happiness. To be sure, different people evaluate different kinds of pleasure differently. The greatest pleasure belongs to those whose goodness is the greatest, since pleasure is related to its source, or to the objects whose attainment creates satisfaction and happiness. Yet Aristotle wants us to realize that there is a distinction between pleasure and happiness in the strict sense of the term, even though for him happiness too is a kind of pleasure. The distinction between pleasure and happiness derives from Aristotle's fundamental point that happiness proper pertains only to the activity of contemplation, which has a trans-political character. This is what Aristotle means when he says that pleasure completes the activity. Pleasure pertains to different activities and we can thus speak of the pleasure related to thought and contemplation. Pleasure related to thought is superior to pleasure related to other activities because of the superiority of thought and the superiority of the objects which thought refers to. There is something divine in thought which assigns to it and to the pleasure associated with it the status of superiority.

Since Aristotle relates happiness to an activity, he has to qualify the scope of the activity. Human beings are incapable of continuous activity; pleasure is therefore not continuous either. Aristotle suggests, on the one hand, that the broad genus for happiness is pleasure and satisfaction. But on the other hand he tries to show happiness' specific feature by not letting it become submerged in the broad meaning of pleasure. The way open to Aristotle is precisely to relate happiness to the activity supporting or engendering it. The ladder-like structure of activities is prescribed by the activities themselves, that is to say, thought is an activity superior to the activity of the senses. Yet Aristotle's correlation of happiness with an activity has two consequences: first, a man is not simply happy by accident – he achieves happiness through an activity and happiness is the outcome of an activity; secondly, happiness

---

[2] *The Politics of Aristotle*, 1264b.

cannot be a continuous state since it is inherent in human activities which are not continuous.[3]

Looking at Aristotle's view of happiness retrospectively by using some of Kant's distinctions which will be explored presently, we may say that Aristotle does not relate happiness to a total harmony between man and the world. This is precluded in Aristotle because the activity of thought and contemplation does not contain harmony, but – precisely what might be called, in subsequent philosophical terminology – intentionality. Intentionality maintains thought and its object in their respective positions. Happiness relates to thought since only thought can refer adequately to metaphysical objects like pure form or the first mover. The level of thought, and concurrently the level of its objects, produces happiness. Happiness is the awareness of thought's achievement of adequate intentionality. The philosopher will be happier than any other person because he exercises and cultivates his reason. Insofar as Aristotle refers to God in this context, he says that the gods should delight in human activity, and regard those who love and honor it. Happiness is not a state of affairs created by human deeds or expectations, because it pertains to the thinking of objects and those objects are present first since they are the metaphysical essence of reality. We may therefore conclude that in Aristotle happiness is the outcome of thinking. It cannot be an aspiration to reach a new stage in the progress of the world. It is eventually related to the structure of thinking characterized by the distinction between subject and object.[4]

3

The concept of levels of pleasure and happiness reemerges in Spinoza although he formulates it somewhat differently, and perhaps even gives it a new meaning. This must be admitted in spite of the fact that Spinoza largely

---

[3] See on the various analyses contained in *The Nicomachean Ethics of Aristotle*, 1095ff.; Book VIII of Ethics, as well as Book X.

On the transformation of the concept 'Eudaimonia' consult Olof Gigon's Introduction to his edition of *Die Nikomachische Ethik*, Eingeleitet und übersetzt von Olaf Gigon, Artemis Verlag, Zürich, 1951, p. 7ff.

[4] The introduction of distinctions and grades into the situation of happiness finds its expression in the terminology applied. A case in point is the distinction between *beatitudo* and *felicitas*. An echo of this distinction is Kant's distinction between *Glückseligkeit* and *Seligkeit* (as to the latter see *Kr. d. p. V.*, p. 137, 142, note 148; transl., p. 123, 128 note, 133.) Seligkeit refers to eternity, p. 148, p. 133, or else to a complete independence from inclinations and needs (p. 137; p. 123).

follows the Aristotelian doctrine on this particular issue.[5] Thus, for instance
in proposition XXIV, Schol. of the Third book of Ethics, Spinoza deals with
the nature of the emotions. He uses the term *bonum* when speaking of the
fact that envy makes a person enjoy another person's predicament, and feel
aggrieved about the good circumstances (*cuiusdem bono*) in which that person
finds himself. Some translators render the term "bonum" as happiness or
felicity, but it should be observed that the term *felicitas* appears explicitly in
Proposition XVIII, Schol. of the Fourth Book, where, Spinoza says, that
since reason makes no demands which are contrary to nature, reason demands
that every man should love himself and seek that which is useful to him.
Spinoza goes on to say that a man should seek what is really useful to him,
or that which really brings him to greater perfection, and that he should
endeavour as far as he can to preserve his own being. It follows that virtue
is nothing but action in accordance with the laws of one's own nature. The
concept of *conatus* reappears in this context; according to Proposition IX
of the Third Book *conatus* is related to the endeavour to persist in its being
for an indefinite period. When this endeavour refers to the mind alone, it
is called will; when it refers to the mind and the body together, it is called
appetite. It follows, that a man enjoys a virtue to the extent that he endea-
vours and can maintain his utility or his being. In Proposition XXI, Spinoza
uses the term *beatum*, stating that nobody can seek to be happy, to do a
good deed, and to live a good life unless he also seeks to live, to be active
and to live. Happiness, in this sense once again refers to the factor described
by Spinoza as *conatus; conatus* is only the existent essence of a thing. Happiness, as related to *conatus* describes the reference of a thing to itself. This
is why Wolfson has rightly observed that *conatus* in this context amounts to
what philosophical systems preceding Spinoza called "natural love." It is
clear from the reference to Spinoza's various propositions that insofar as
they are related to the *conatus*, happiness or pleasure designates the very
persistence of a thing. The activity refers here to existence, being both carried
by an existing thing and referring to it. It is not an activity designed to attain
a particular goal. This sort of activity is not therefore presented in a scale in
the Aristotelian manner. Insofar as pleasure is concerned, it can be said that
pleasure is simply the enjoyment of existence.

   Spinoza's second level of happiness is related to the highest state of intellectual cognition. The Third Chapter of his *Theological-political Treatise*

---

[5] On the Aristotelian tradition and Spinoza's indebtedness to it consult: Harry Austryn
Wolfson, *The Philosophy of Spinoza*, Vol. II, New York, Schocken, 1958, p. 233ff. On the
norms implied in Spinoza's distinction see the present author's: Conatus and Amor Dei.
The total and the partial norm, *Revue Internationale de Philosophie*, 1977, pp. 117 ff.

already refers to wisdom and cognition of the truth as the source of man's true happiness, and as is well-known, this notion is central to the last propositions of the Ethics, where Spinoza refers to delight, the highest possible mental acquiescence, our salvation, blessedness, etc. Spinoza hesitates about using the term pleasure in this context. The character of blessedness with all its nuances is emphasized by the statement that the mind is less subject to evil emotions and fears death less on the level of intellectual cognition. Here we are no longer talking about existence and endurance but about perfection proper, and there is a clear correlation or proportion between perfection and activity: activity is fully achieved only on the level of cognition.

For Aristotle, happiness is the result which accompanies cognition. Aristotle did not employ the notion of reward there because happiness or blessedness in an outcome of an activity and cannot be placed in the context of rewards. Spinoza on the other hand explicitly comes back to the notion of reward (*praemium*), speaking now about *beatitudo* or blessedness. In Proposition XLII of the Fifth Book he says that blessedness is not the reward of virtue but virtue itself. Blessedness consists of love for God, and therefore arises from the highest kind of cognition. This is an important point since, even though he introduces the notion of blessedness, Spinoza seems to be going even further than Aristotle. Blessedness is not concomitant to the highest achievement on the scale of cognition; it is that very cognition. The highest virtue is the knowledge of God, and at the same time this virtue is blessedness. Spinoza does not indicate a conceptual distinction between blessedness and virtue as such by suggesting that the highest level of knowledge is in itself the highest achievement. It cannot be translated into terms which describe the human response or enjoyment of the achievement. Both Aristotle and Spinoza indicate a relation, or even correlation, between cognition and happiness: for Aristotle happiness is a result of cognition, while for Spinoza cognition and happiness coincide. There is an aspect to the achievement of the mind in its highest manifestation which relates to character, since man's ability to control his emotions depends solely on the understanding. There is a human response to blessedness because human beings rejoice in their blessedness. This situation brings about the characterological outcome: no one rejoices in blessedness because he has controlled his lusts; on the contrary the ability to control lust arises from blessedness itself. True knowledge has an effect on human emotions. The question to be asked, which has not been asked by Spinoza himself is: what will be the relation between blessedness on the level of knowledge and pleasure on the level of *conatus* be? The highest level of knowledge is destined to be the controlling stage of human life. But, because of his concern with the question of the relation between emotions and the intellect, Spinoza failed to deal with the broader aspect of the relation between existence, endurance and knowledge.

Be that as it may, there is a systematic attempt in Spinoza to use the notions of activity and blessedness. Here again, to anticipate that our subsequent exploration of Kant's notion of happiness, we must note that happiness does not relate to a new condition of the universe, a condition in which human activity will be fully harmonious with the state of nature or in which the state of nature will be structured according to human expectations. In both Aristotle and Spinoza happiness proper refers to cognition, and cognition, by definition, does not create a new state of reality. It only conceives of the given reality insofar as given reality connotes the ultimate structure of reality or its ultimate principles. Instead of envisaging a new reality, a top level of knowledge is posited. The achievement does not indicate an ontological structure of reality which is an overriding harmony, but climbing the ladder of cognition. The intellectual character of the ideal of happiness comes to the fore in two interrelated issues (a) the highest human achievement is the highest level of knowledge, (b) only through the highest level of knowledge does man find himself or achieve a state of happiness or blessedness. Happiness or blessedness is related to the discerning quality of knowledge, and not to the anticipatory character of human deeds and their end. It is at this point that Kant introduces a new version of the concept of happiness. But, before moving to an investigation of Kant's notion, we must turn our attention to the notion of happiness presented in Utilitarian philosophy. We are disregarding the chronological order here since we are concerned with a typological investigation of different notions of happiness. The Utilitarian view of the concept of happiness might be seen, at least partially, as a variation on the theme of happiness related to day-to-day existence. Hence a short comment on the notion of utility and happiness is apposite at this juncture.

4

In the Utilitarian system there is an identification, or what appears to be an identification, between happiness and pleasure, and between these and what goes by the name of utility. The point of departure for the Utilitarian version of the notion of happiness is the assumption that nature has put mankind under the government of two masters, pain and pleasure.[6] The

---

[6] See: Jeremy Bentham, *An Introduction to The Principles of Morals and Legislation*, Hafner, New York, 1948, p. 1, 70, 267, 312.

principle of happiness, or utility, recognizes or does not recognize an action according to whether it exhibits the tendency to increase or decrease the happiness of those who have an interest in it. The principle of utility is therefore a principle which measures the promotion of happiness or the tendency to prevent it. Happiness is identical or synonymous with pleasure, benefit, enjoyment or goodness. Since happiness is implied in the actual life of human beings, the principle of happiness becomes a principle relevant to the life of society. Preference is therefore given to increasing happiness rather than to attempting to decrease it. The principle of happiness or utility thus recognizes the natural tendency to seek pleasure and shun pain. Since nature prescribes the course of action, the latter can be left to human interest, which leads to pleasure. Nature prescribes the agent of action and the object of action – the self-same human being is aware of his interest and of his goal.

John Stuart Mill comes back to the same considerations, although his presentation differs from that of Jeremy Bentham. Mill grants that happiness is an ultimate end, but questions relating to ultimate ends are not amenable to direct proof. Since ultimate ends cannot be proven, we are only left with the possibility of proving that something is a means to something else which is affirmed to be good without proof. Pleasure is taken as an ultimate end, and actions are right to the extent that they tend to promote happiness; they are wrong inasmuch as they tend to produce the absence of pleasure, or the reverse of happiness. But Mill nevertheless comes back to the Aristotelian notion of grades or kinds of pleasure; some kinds are more desirable and more valuable than others. We cannot rely on nature in its broad sense, and have to refer to human nature or human aspirations. Beasts' pleasures do not satisfy a human being's conception of happiness. Once human beings are made conscious of their faculties they do not regard anything as happiness which does not give them gratification. This is why Mill stated in his famous phrase that it is better to be Socrates dissatisfied than a fool satisfied. Mill remains within the concept of nature but he introduces variations in the scope of happiness, which eventually lead him to an ambiguous position whereby satisfaction of human faculties accounts for the diversity and scale of human activities; the more human an activity is, the more satisfactory it can be. Satisfaction is a human response to an activity, and thus has a re-flexive character. But there are nevertheless objective criteria which direct the gradation of human activities; satisfaction is a response not only to what man does, but also to what he is expected to do.[7]

---

[7] Consult: John Stuart Mill, Utilitarianism, in *Utilitarianism, Liberty, Representative Government*, introduction by A.D. Lindsay, London, J.M. Dent & Sons Ltd., New York, E.P. Dutton & Co. Inc., 1960.

We have dealt with three types of approach to the concept of happiness. What is characteristic of all of them, is that they relate happiness to human activities, seeing it as a response rooted in these activities. This response is sometimes viewed as a new situation for the agent involved in the activities. The various types of interpretation of the notion of happiness also provide a scale of happiness, whether this is introduced directly as in Aristotle and Spinoza, or indirectly as in Mill.

Having established a frame of reference for our analysis, we can move on to Kant's notion of happiness.

5

According to Aristotle and Spinoza, happiness is related to the consummation of knowledge. In Aristotle and Spinoza, as an effect of knowledge or as its reward, happiness is attainable for the peak of knowledge is attainable. Kant cuts the ground from under the very possibility of a conjunction of knowledge and happiness. Kant conceives of reason as the highest intellectual faculty. But precisely because of this, reason (*Vernunft*) cannot refer to objects or to intuitions, but only to understanding and its propositions. Reason, placed at this highest level, does not connote a stage of knowledge characterized by fullness or fulfilment. Within reason proper there is no contact between the idea and the lofty object of knowledge; they are not adequate to one another – and it is immaterial whether the object is conceived in the Aristotelian sense as pure form or as prime mover, or in Spinoza's sense as God *qua* total substance. Since there are no objects of this kind within the boundaries of reason, reason cannot reach them. Thus the presupposition for happiness is lacking, i.e. the final achievement of reason. Kant does not relate happiness to knowledge and its consummation but moves it to the realm of the satisfaction of human inclinations and urges. While traditional views, particularly Aristotle, relate satisfaction to different human activities, Kant relates happiness *qua* satisfaction to human inclinations. He is led to the conclusion that this satisfaction cannot be achieved or safeguarded.

A different version of the same point can be rendered referring to the concept of the non-sensuous intuition or of what Kant calls intellectual intuition (*Intellektuelle Anschauung*). The noumenon in Kant's view is not and cannot be an object of sensuous intuition. We can understand the noumenon as the object of a suprasensuous intuition, once we assume a mode of intuition which is not our mode of intuition and the possibilities of which we cannot understand.[8] Moreover, he who considers himself in possession of this kind of intuition is inclined to despise and to belittle understanding, whose way of knowing the world is discursive. A philosophy which employs this kind of intuition is not engaged in work, but considers itself noble and lofty (*vornehm*).[9] Our knowledge requires a synthesis of understanding and intuition. The divine intellect is an intellect endowed with intuition. It is an intellect which does not represent given objects to itself, but, by representing objects, the objects themselves are given or created.[10] The outcome of this argument is that if happiness is related to the peak of knowledge when the peak of knowledge is beyond our reach, happiness too is beyond our reach. The peak is a model of the divine intellect, but happiness is not associated with the divine intellect: in the Aristotelian view happiness is an achievement, or the result of an activity, but the divine intellect is not engaged in activity and achievement. The peak embodied in divine knowledge is there from the beginning: the divine intellect does not disclose objects – it creates them. On the other hand, within the boundaries of human understanding, understanding is not accompanied by happiness because of the limitations inherent in that understanding. Happiness cannot be present in the human realm because of its limitations, while in the divine realm happiness cannot be present because of its lack of limitations. The result of this analysis is that in Kant, unlike in his predecessors, happiness is not correlated with knowledge. We can even go further and say that the ideal of knowledge *ipso facto* does not have a moral standing. The traditional combination of knowledge and happiness gave knowledge a moral status. By differentiating between these two aspects, Kant re-emphasizes the confinement of knowledge to itself; insofar as happiness connotes a moral quality, it has to be looked for somewhere else.

In traditional systems the noble position of knowledge has a cognitive correlate in the noble position of the objects of knowledge, be they ideas, pure form, or God. In Kant on the other hand knowledge refers to objects of experience. Knowledge is the sum-total of representations unified by forms of understanding. There is no noble quality or attribute to the objects; consequently objects cannot give knowledge the status of an intellectual ideal or of a moral ideal implied in the intellectual one. Kant says of himself in the famous confession, "my place is the fruitful *bathos* of experience." Following this we can say, by way of a play on words using their Greek roots, that the knowledge which refers to experience lacks "*pathos*," that is to say,

---

[8] *Kr.d.r.V.*, B, p. 307; p. 268.

[9] Von einem neuerdings erhobenen Ton in der Philosophie (1796), in *Immanuel Kants Werke*, ed. E. Cassirer, Band VI, Berlin, Bruno Cassirer, 1914, p. 478ff.

[10] *Kr.d.r.V.*, B, p. 145; p. 161.

the elevation implied in the achievement of happiness. Whether or not
Kant's understanding of the meaning of happiness changed is a question to
be explored. What is already clear from the point of view of the outline of
the system is that happiness cannot retain the status it enjoyed within the
context suggested by Aristotle and Spinoza.

Let us now look into some of Kant's definitions or presentations of the
concept of happiness. Happiness, says Kant, is the rational beings' consciousness of the agreeableness of life (*Annehmlichkeit des Lebens*) which
accompanies his whole existence, without interruption.[11] This definition
stresses the relation of happiness to rational beings: only a rational being
is endowed with consciousness, and happiness presupposes consciousness
and its response. Happiness is not an opaque situation but a kind of understanding that a situation is agreeable. In addition, as we see, Kant emphasizes
the continuity, the uninterruptedness of the situation. It therefore follows
from the negative point of view that instantaneous satisfaction or pleasure
cannot be viewed as happiness. We have seen in our previous explorations
that Aristotle presented happiness precisely as a situation which is not
constant and it is understandable that Aristotle took this line: if happiness
is related to an activity, and if there is no continuous activity, happiness,
too, cannot have an uninterrupted character. Kant's presentation of the
very meaning of happiness implies a question: he defines happiness in a way
which enables him to argue that it is beyond the reach of the rational beings'
involvement in experience, since experience has a fleeting character: it occurs
against the background of time, and even permanence is an interpretation of
time, while lack of interruption points to a situation beyond experience and
beyond time. In the context in which Kant defines the essence of happiness,
he immediately adds a comment which can only be read as downgrading the
status of happiness: The principle, he says, of making happiness the supreme
ground of volition is a principle of self-love (*Selbstliebe*).[12] Happiness is not
only presented architectonically as transcending experience, but morally as
a version of egoism. This is because the achievement of happiness refers to
the agent and not to his fellow-man, and *a fortiori* not to the totality of human beings. In his *Metaphysik der Sitten*, Kant refers to the Eudaimonist
who thinks that happiness is a moral idea.[13] Kant does not emphasize the
continuous character of happiness, and even self-love is manifest only in the
tranquility of the soul and in the satisfaction derived from the moral deed.
If this is so, then Kant's evaluation of happiness in this context is quite close

[11] *Kr.d.pr.Ver.*, p. 25; p. 21.
[12] *Ibid.*
[13] *Met.d.S.*, p. 208.

to that present in Stoicism and in Cicero. The definition of the Eudaimonist leads to a criticism of the stand he takes; the direction of the criticism is that the Eudaimonist is not so much concerned with the moral deed as with the satisfaction it produces. From this point of view the Eudaimonist combines the moral deed with achievement for the benefit of the doer, though Kant does not in this context refer to achievement as self-love.

A slightly different aspect of happiness emerges here. Happiness amounts to a state of *"Wohlbefinden,"* but this is not external or accidental and does not depend upon experience but on our own choice. Kant speaks of happiness as a state of satisfaction; the point he is trying to make is that the circumstances surrounding man do not live up to his expectations, as we have seen, he emphasizes the uninterrupted harmony between expectations and circumstances. Emphasis shifts from circumstances, since circumstances involve an empirical, and thus an accidental, ingredient. Hence Kant attempts to present a possibility for happiness independent of changing empirical conditions. The shift is from the environment to the *"Gesinnungen"* of the doer. But as is well known, the *Gesinnungen* are the very essence of morality. It is in this sense that Kant says that happiness is not the greatest sum of pleasure, but the satisfaction which emerges from man's consciousness of controlling himself – (*Bewusstsein seiner Selbstmacht, zufrieden zu sein*). It seems plausible to understand that description as implying the state of tranquility of the soul referred to before. But the main emphasis is on man controlling himself, self-control is eventually an act of choice or of will. Hence satisfaction depends on the choice of the agent rather than on a correspondence between the agent and the circumstances of his existence.

Our enquiry has led us to the conclusion that insofar as morality is a manifestation of reason in its purity, it cannot assume happiness as a ground of determination for moral conduct. Pure reason *per se* does not contain a correspondence between its own principles and the surrounding conditions. The definition of happiness as a harmony between human desires or expectations and reality points to nature as reality. Thus it points to an extra-moral realm. This notion can be put differently: since morality amounts to obedience of a pure moral law, morality cannot relate to occurrences in the world. This is so because there exists a fundamental dichotomy between those occurrences which are by definition occurrences in the realm of the senses and moral legislation. Once the law is the determining ground of the will, happiness cannot be viewed as a moral goal. Thus, from the point of view of the relation between will, morality and reason, as well as from the point of view of the position of the law which is systematically different from the position of an object and of a goal, Kant could not allocate happiness a systematic moral position either with respect to principle or with respect to end.

Yet, when we look closely into the different texts we find that Kant was somehow dissatisfied with these systematic or architectonic arguments relating to the position of happiness within the orbit of morality. Kant put forward additional arguments. We have to look into them mainly because they bring us closer to the notion of the Primacy of Practical Reason. Kant intended this idea, among other things, to overcome the initial antithesis between morality or the moral law and happiness. It was meant to lend concreteness to the striving to achieve a harmony between expectations and reality.

6

Kant rejects the moral validity of happiness not only because the notion of happiness turns the deed into a means instead of an end, but also because happiness runs counter to the universalistic aspect of morality. Happiness, even of everybody, is a situation in which the individual as such enjoys happiness. Happiness is a personal or self-referential status. Happiness of all can be a *post factum* summation but not a universality or a kingdom established in the first place. Even when we refer to the happiness of our fellow man, we shift our concern from the acknowledgement of our fellow man to recognition of a state of happiness he is to realize. The self-referential and thus eventually egotistic aspect of happiness prevents it from becoming a universal moral law. Suppose that I take it upon myself to foster my fellow man's happiness; in that case I am motivated by the recognition of my fellow man and only indirectly by the happiness to which he aspires. Thus it is the obligation of universality which is implied vis-à-vis our fellow man, and not the direct approach to happiness as such. Since happiness is understood as self-love, there is an intrinsic contradiction between the content and direction of self-love and the universality of the moral law. It is clear that Kant is indirectly taking issue with utilitarianism and its principle, viz. the happiness of all. And it is obvious that Kant's understanding of universality, which cannot be viewed as the sum-total of scattered individuals each one enjoying happiness as a state of affairs in the midst of which he is placed, is paramount here. Universality connotes the subjection of the agent to a trans-egotistical law; the objective of universality is to establish a realm of agents, whose *ratio essendi* will not accrue to the agents. Kant attempts to reinforce this consideration by referring the striving for happiness to inclinations, and inclinations are not the proper ground for morality to begin with. Because happiness depends on inclinations, happiness belongs to cleverness (*Klug-heit*) but not to wisdom (*Weisheit*).[14]

All this amounts to an emphasis on the incompatibility of happiness as a moral end and the sphere of morality proper, an incompatibility which is due both to the nature of happiness and to the nature of the moral law. But Kant goes further in his criticism of the moral status of happiness; we may put the direction of his criticism in this context as a kind of empirical incompatibility between happiness and the sphere of morality.

Happiness is not only self-referential in terms of the agent; it is subjective or, let us say, relative as well. Each individual interprets happiness from his own particular position and point of view. Happiness depends on individual feelings. This is so because happiness is by definition a kind of pleasure; it is impossible to anticipate the individual response of pleasure to a situation *a priori*. Moreover, happiness varies not only from individual to individual, but also in the same individual in different situations according to his means of satisfying him. There is no way of predicting the nature of happiness *a priori*. Experience alone can tell us what eventually produces joy, pleasure and happiness in us. It is experience lifted by induction to a level of generality or universality, and the attempt to argue that there is a rational argument which can establish happiness is pseudo-rationality (*vernünfteln*).[15] The gist of Kant's argument in this context is that happiness is essentially a vague concept because of its individual, subjective and erratic character. The reference to given situations probably served to underline the basic notion that any material rendering of moral principles undermines the universality of morality.

Once we realize the relation between happiness and empirical conditions, we have to realize also that happiness changes with different historical periods; even in the same period happiness differs according to the conditions obtaining in different social strata (Kant uses a play on words here: *Stände und Umstände*). The changing character of happiness conforms to the conceptions and habits of different individuals in different conditions of life. This is an additional aspect of the relative character of happiness, relative – in this case – to historical periods and concrete conditions of life. In any case, the reference to the empirical ingredients of happiness is meant to emphasize the fundamental impossibility of introducing happiness into the context of moral considerations, once moral considerations are grounded in reason and removed from empirical states of mind.

---

[14] *Kr.d.pr.V.*, p. 129; 115.
[15] *Met.d.S.*, p. 14.

Kant produces another argument which can be rendered as follows: happiness can be conceived of as related to human desires and inclinations, but human nature defies the very possibility of achieving happiness as satisfaction. Human nature prompts man to look for new properties and new pleasures; man's desires go beyond any possibility of satisfying them. It is because of this aspect of human nature, that human beings have aspirations and strivings; these are more important to them than any achieved goal. Of course, happiness is an achieved goal. But there is an additional obstacle: man is dragged into misfortunes of his own making by the discord among his inner natural tendencies, such as the oppression of power and the barbarism of wars. These natural tendencies eventually lead to misery and thus to a clash between man's expectation of achieving happiness and of the satisfaction with his own deeds which undermines that expectation.[16] Kant takes in this context human nature in two senses: human nature entails expectations; but it also entails the forces which make it impossible to fulfill expectations. Because of human nature's double face, it cannot be the basis of morality. What emerges, therefore, from this part of Kant's analysis is not only that there is a discrepancy between morality and happiness, but also that happiness occupies a shaky position which makes it impossible and inconceivable to base morality – and even human goals – on the vague notion of happiness.

7

We have already had to refer to the notion of human nature and its basic contradiction: its simultaneous striving to achieve satisfaction and inability to achieve it. It is clear that Kant uses the term "nature" in the context of human nature rather vaguely. If nature is to be understood as the existence of things determined according to universal laws, then it seems obvious that Kant is employing the term nature in the context of human nature and happiness in a way which is not fully consonant with this definition. The use of the term nature in the context of human nature, is close to Kant's use of it when he speaks e.g. of our natural inclination toward metaphysics, or when he refers to the nature of reason. Indeed, Kant uses the term "*Naturanlage*" for metaphysics, and also for man or human nature.[17] But once the broad concept of nature has been introduced, an additional aspect of happiness comes to the fore. Happiness cannot accrue to man, since, as far as man is concern-

---

[16] *Kr.d.U.*, p. 299f.; *part* à, p. 93f.
[17] *Prolegomena*, § 60.

ed, nature wanted man to create whatever goes beyond the animal order of
reality for himself. Hence, man will not have a share in happiness or in
perfection except insofar as he himself produces it. Since he is free from
instinctual determination, he will do this by reason alone. Hence, Kant adds,
it is not in the interest of reason to allow man to live contentedly (*wohl lebe*).
It has been in the interest of reason to let human nature work itself out; and
in every work of man he will reach the place which his behaviour will make
him worthy for life in a situation of well-being (*Wohlbefinden*).[18] Hence,
and this is eventually Kant's point, if it were nature's objective that man
should enjoy happiness, reason would not be the most adequate means of
achieving this goal. Instincts would better fulfill this function. The inner
necessity of desires and instincts, cannot anthropologically speaking, fulfill
the function of reason. Kant refers instincts to the faculty of producing the
desire to control and possess objects even before we know about the objects.
The examples he quotes are the sexual instinct and the parental instinct
which leads animals to protect their offspring.[19]

We can summarize this by saying that nature in its cosmic sense has not
granted man the possibility of achieving what he wants to achieve and what
he has to achieve by the force of nature itself. Man is destined to achieve
what he wants to achieve through his own activity; this is the meaning of
Kant's reference in the *Kritik der Urteilskraft* §83 to the distinction between
happiness and culture. Man is not guided by his instinctual equipment, and
this equipment in fact falls short of human goals. But, Kant thought that
man's natural inclination is nevertheless to desire to achieve happiness. In
his criticism of Stoic moral philosophy Kant argues that the mistake the
Stoics made is that they did not include man's happiness as well as his virtues
in the notion of the supreme good. The Stoics, Kant argues, placed happiness
in the act itself and in the satisfaction of man's personal worthiness, and
thus submerged happiness in the moral mode of thinking about human
being.[20] The following would be an adequate interpretation of the point
Kant is making against the Stoa: The Stoics failed to see that happiness
refers to the human situation as a harmony between man and his surround-
ings. They shifted happiness from man's position in the surrounding world
to man's inward state, and his inwardness, as Kant puts it, is the moral mode
of thinking. But according to Kant, this direction is unrealizable, because
the voice of nature, the voice of their own nature, defies the Stoic system.
It is clear that the reference to human nature is here a reference to a legiti-

---

[18] Idea for a Universal History, *On History*, p. 14.
[19] *Anthropologie*, § 78, p. 128.
[20] *Kr.d.pr.V.*, p. 145ff; p. 131ff. See the Excursus at the end of the present book.

mate authority, at least insofar as the supreme good is concerned. In terms of that good we cannot be oblivious of what nature aspires to achieve, in spite of the fact that nature cannot achieve its goal, and in spite of the fact that natural forces cannot lead man to it. Man's worthiness to achieve happiness is the link between present human behaviour in accordance with the principles of reason and the achievement of happiness which is a goal, though an unattainable one. Hence it is our next task to deal with the concept of man's worthiness for happiness.

8

Kant already considers man's worthiness to be happy the maximum which can be obtained within the boundaries of theoretical reason in the *Critique of Pure Reason:* do that which makes thee worthy of happiness.[21] The actual attainment of happiness goes beyond theoretical reason. This is why Kant pushes his point to the very threshold of the practical by limiting the statement in terms of pure reason and its practical interest to the notion of being worthy of happiness. But we must observe that by indicating happiness, even though he limits its achievement to worthiness as a pre-condition of the state of happiness, Kant is clearly going beyond the scope of theory and expects, envisages, or has a practical fulfilment in mind. The very expectation of attaining happiness, and the activity leading to this expectation implied in the notion of worthiness already transcend strictly theoretical considerations. The whole man, as it were, considers himself worthy of happiness and anticipates the state of being happy. While Kant somehow overburdens the analysis of theoretical reason by imposing the relation to happiness on it, he sometimes tends to use the same concept of worthiness in his ethical analysis when he says that morality is not a doctrine about how we can be happy but a doctrine about how we can be worthy of happiness. From the point of view of theoretical reason Kant related being worthy of happiness to practical interest. Now, when it comes to the exploration of practical happiness he promotes the idea of happiness again by making morality the *conditio sine qua non* only for being worthy of attaining happiness.

A similar consideration comes to the fore in Kant's suggestion about the relation between ethical theory and religion, since, as Kant says, religion represents the dimension of hope. Religion employs the concept of a creator of the world identical not only with benevolence but with complete goodness.

---

[21] *Kr.d.r.V.*, p. 837; p. 638.

The hope entertained is that the creator of the world will eventually bring about harmony between morality in the strict sense of the term and the expectation of happiness. The good creator of the world will produce and safeguard the conjunction of these two different ingredients: the morality of the rational being and happiness. Because of the systematic consideration which upholds the distinction between morality and happiness within the moral realm itself, and because worthiness is the maximum which can be attained both in the theoretical and in the moral realm, – Kant introduces the notion of Postulates. Postulates are not presuppositions of practical reason and *a fortiori* are not presuppositions of theoretical reason. Postulates are statements about anticipated complementary situations, where the openness of the sphere of theory and the openness of the sphere of morality are rounded off. Because morality and happiness do not coincide, the Postulates indicate a situation of harmony and coincidence between morality, the expectation of attaining happiness and happiness as such. Postulates transcend not only the boundaries of theoretical reason, but also those of practical reason. The exploration of theoretical reason transfers the practical interest to morality. In the sphere of morality, happiness, as a situation which responds to worthiness, is once more transposed beyond morality proper into a postulated, i.e. harmonious, cosmos where the parallel lines of morality and happiness eventually coincide. We are concerned here with Kant's notion of the Primacy of Practical Reason inasmuch as it indicates a solution to problems left open in the theoretical sphere. We arrive at the paradoxical conclusion that the problem of happiness which emerges on the level of theoretical reason does not find its solution on the level of practical reason either. This is because on this level Kant is led to a distinction between legislation and expectation. Legislation, which is characteristic of practical reason, solves the problem of freedom but does not solve the problem of happiness. To solve the problem of happiness Kant had to establish an additional level beside practical reason qua legislation. Postulates are not laws; they are statements related to an envisaged future. Happiness is part of Kant's vision but not part of his ethical theory.

This is reinforced by pointing out that Kant does not hesitate to use the notion of grace when speaking of the relation between attaining happiness and grace. Grace is a gift from the supreme being; here Kant does not even refer to worthiness but to receptivity (*Empfänglichkeit*) on the part of the man who will partake of this happiness.[22] The fact that Kant uses the notion of grace here places the whole investigation in Leibniz' conceptual frame-

---

[22] *Religion*, p. 70, note.

work, i.e. the idea of harmony between the kingdom of nature and the kingdom of grace. This is so in spite of the fact that Kant took issue with Leibniz on the question of theodicy.[23] Kant, who could not agree with Leibniz about the possibility of a theodicy since he assumed that finite beings cannot understand harmony, replaced the idea of theodicy with the idea of the postulate or expectation. The expectation is warranted, but knowledge of the situation envisaged in the expectation is unattainable. Thus it does not belong to practical reason and autonomy, let alone to theoretical reason. It belongs to a utopia in which all courses of action will achieve their consummation in total harmony.

9

We can at this point summarize Kant's problem vis-à-vis happiness and the solution he proposes.[24]

Let us put it negatively first: Kant could not follow one of the traditional lines, in which happiness is a pleasure presented on a scale of levels of pleasure. The reason for this is to be found in his ethical theory, where there are no levels of ethical behaviour. There is only *one* level of ethical behaviour, the level of universality or, to put it negatively, the level at which self-love is overcome.

Furthermore, Kant could not follow another traditional line, which saw happiness as a reward for an activity, because the very notion of a reward would defy the universalization inherent in the ethical activity. Happiness amounts to self-love, and thus runs counter to other components in Kant's theory: (*a*) that there is no room for rewards at all, since universalization is both the content of an ethical deed and its motive, and (*b*) a reward is by definition a situation which benefits the agent and thus undermines the self-contained character of the universal ethical imperative.

Nor could Kant follow the third possibility of presenting happiness as a consequence of intellectual activity. Kant could not accept this since there

---

[23] Über das Misslingen aller philosophischen Versuche der Theodicee, Kirchmann's edition of *Kants Sämmtliche Werke*, Leipzig, Verlag der Dürrschen Buchhandlung, n.d., Vol. VI, p. 144ff.

[24] On the notion of happiness compare the previously quoted article by Yirmiahu Yovel, The Highest Good and History in Kant's Thought, *Archiv für Geschichte der Philosophie*, 54. Band, 1972, Heft 3, p. 238ff.

On the concept of the Primacy of Practical Reason see the present author's:

(1) *Experience and its Systematization: Studies in Kant*, 2nd edition, Martinus Nijhoff, The Hague, 1972, p. 111ff. (2) *On the Human Subject: Studies in the Phenomenology of Ethics and Politics*, Springfield, Illinois, Charles C. Thomas, 1966, p. 134ff.

is no bliss to the intellectual activity. The active character of knowledge in Kant, which amounts to the unifying and structuring character of the intellect, removes the possibility of connecting intellectual activity with discerning something essential, removed or hidden. Thus the satisfaction connected with intellectual activity is missing when it amounts to imposing forms on data, and not to reading ideas of essences.

On the positive side, this is what emerges: Kant conceives of happiness as a constant situation, and here, at least implicitly takes exception to Aristotle. A constant situation is one where there is full harmony between expectations and circumstances. Thus, for Kant, the centre of gravity shifts from the activity to the state of affairs. The activity is that of making oneself worthy of the state of affairs, but it does not produce the state of affairs. The state of affairs in this sense has to be grounded in the structure of the universe. Nature can not be the *locus* for the fulfilment of expectation. Nature in the envisaged sense of the Postulates is a totality which transcends the concept of nature as understood in theoretical reason: there nature is either the sum-total of data or the sum-total of laws, but not a self-contained and rounded totality. Paradoxically, from the point of view of practical reason and ethical theory, there is no room for the concept of nature from the outset. Practical reason is productive reason or self-legislating reason, and as such is totally separate from data and the structure of categories under which they are subsumed. From the point of view of practical reason Kant could not address himself to the realm of nature at all. Kant transposes nature to the realm of ethical theory only because it is a concept or a problem within the boundaries of theoretical reason. He now interprets nature as a totality which as such is capable of responding to the expectations assumed in his ethical theory. Kant was aware of the fact that the various versions of happiness occupied a central place in traditional theories. He was unable to put happiness in the hard-core of his ethical theory and therefore assumed its position as a Postulate in the terminological sense of that concept. But by doing so, he gave it the far-reaching connotation of a total state of affairs, which makes it even less accessible than it had been in terms of the traditional theories. Since Kant could not absorb the notion of happiness systematically he presented a sort of utopia of happiness, which amounts to a harmony between the worthy man and a constant state of affairs.

The following ingredients are present in Kant's notion of happiness and in the systematic translation of that notion into a postulate: first, there is the worthiness of the agent. Inasmuch as he is worthy he remains within the confines of his deed, but somehow looks beyond these confines to what is sup-

posed to happen to him. This look becomes expectation or hope; worthiness is
turned into a positive attitude which implies that the worthy agent will not
expect in vain. The positive attitude becomes a postulate according to which
the agent not only legitimately expects a reward but also postulates the attainment of the reward. This calls for the creation of a universe in which
worthiness is complemented by a situation suited to the worthy agent. The
whole spectrum is thus moved from the agent's introspection to the structure of the universe.

10

Precisely because our study is concerned with the place of empirical human
behaviour in Kant's practical philosophy, the issue of happiness and its
variations is significant and symptomatic of the general trend of Kant's
practical philosophy. Why did Kant not incorporate the expectation or the
ideal of happiness in his ethical system? Why did he instead relegate it to the
Postulates with all that goes with the systematic position of the concepts and
the expectations called Postulates? There is probably one major reason for
this which is related to the fact that, as we have seen, happiness has been
viewed in many traditional systems not only as coterminous with day-to-day
human aspirations and hopes, but also as concomitant with the highest level
of human activity; it has been viewed as an ideal, not only as a motive. Here
Kant's basic position clashes with the traditional systems and the centrality
they give happiness. Happiness, even when related to or concomitant with
the highest level of cognition, is an achievement, or a state of affairs, a situation; it thus carries in itself a component of *actio transiens*. Directing
practice to happiness disrupts the immanent self-enclosed character of
morality. Kant interpreted happiness as relating to the harmony between
man and the world, to fulfillment, to the very meeting between man and
what is extra-human. All these components in his analysis or – what might
be described – phenomenology of happiness led him to take the ideal of
happiness out of the sphere delineated by morality in the strict sense of the
term.

Because of this competition in his system, between happiness which connotes
an outcome and the determination by the moral law which connotes an autarchic
character of morality, Kant arrives at a paradoxical conclusion: he does not
turn the – all too human – expectation of happiness into a vehicle for ethical
action, though, as we shall see, he takes many evil human deeds to be vehicles
of that sort. Evil can serve the good, as war can serve peace, or competition

can serve cooperation. But one alleged good, like happiness, is not made subservient to the real good which consists of the purity of the moral imperative. One of the ways in which Kant tries to overcome the rigid dichotomy between the empirical level and the intelligible level is by characterizing the empirical level by results which go beyond intentions. This structure is not applicable to happiness because happiness cannot – phenomenologically speaking – be separated from intentions and expectations and from the human being approving the situation and affirming it as one of happiness. It is precisely because happiness in its own way creates a self-enclosed circle (even though the given situation is a component of the circle) it competes, systematically of philosophically, with the self-enclosed circle delineated by the morality of duty or the morality of freedom.

Ultimately we can render the systematic clash between the two systems as a clash between the morality of the origin and the morality of the end – the former being Kant's system and the latter being the different variations on the ideal of happiness. This is so in spite of the fact that Kant reinforced his moral philosophy as that of origin by presenting the origin as an end, in the sense that the agent motivated by the origin affirms that origin as his ultimate objective and does not look for an achievement or a reward outside the boundaries of the origin as such.

We now turn to aspects of Kant's system which relate to the empirical directions of human behaviour. It will be our task to present and formulate the limitations inherent in harmonizing the pure and the empirical.

CHAPTER THREE

HISTORY AND HARMONIZATION

1

Kant's *Kritik der Urteilskraft* (Critique of Judgement) contains two symmetrical views on the position of war. War is referred to in the aesthetic evaluation on the one hand and in the context of its human consequences on the other.

In the first part of *Kritik der Urteilskraft* Kant deals with war under the heading of the sublime. The sublime is the name given to what is absolutely great, to that which is beyond all comparison in that position.[1] The sublime is that in comparison with which all else is small.[2] But when the concept of sublimity is translated into the disposition of the soul, the sublime is that which demonstrates a faculty of mind transcending every standard of sense.[3] When the sublime object is viewed as overwhelmingly great, it evokes respect, just as contempt is felt in the face of that which we call absolutely small.[4] But sublimity does not imbue the sublime object with the quality of good, and there is no delight in the sublime if there is delight in the good.[5] Since the sublime belongs to the aesthetic sphere, it does not evoke a command, as the absolutely good does, but only what Kant calls "a pure intellectual judgment."[6] (General Remark to para 29, 118).

Kant subsumes the phenomenon of war under the broad concept of sublimity when he says that there is something sublime about it, adding that the more innumerable the dangers to which nations that make war are exposed and which they are able to meet with fortitude, the more sublime their stamp of mind becomes.[7] Sublimity is thus attributed to the phenomenon of war on the one hand and to human fortitude on the other in a way

[1] *Kr.d.U.*, p. 91; p. 94.
[2] *Ibid.*, p. 94; p. 97.
[3] *Ibid.*, p. 94; p. 98.
[4] *Ibid.*, p. 93; p. 96.
[5] *Ibid.*, p. 87; p. 90.
[6] *Ibid.*, p. 113; p. 118.
[7] *Ibid.*, p. 108–109; p. 112–113.

which parallels Kant's location of sublimity in objects on the one hand and in dispositions of the soul on the other. To be sure, when Kant says that war has something sublime about it he adds the moral proviso, that it be conducted with order and with a sacred respect for the rights of civilians. The conjunction of these two elements, order as a general structure of reality and civilian rights as a legal or ethical concept, imposes moral inhibitions on the conduct of war. But this can probably also be understood in the broader sense that only reality which is not chaotic can have a sublime character. That this means that war has to be non-chaotic can perhaps be ascertained from Kant's statement that an ocean, agitated by storms, cannot be called sublime, since it has a horrible aspect.[8] Order, more concretely expressed as respect for human rights and observance of those rights, prevents war from becoming horrible, and is thus a *conditio sine qua non* for the application of the category of sublimity to war. To return to the previously mentioned distinction between sublimity and goodness, it should be reasserted here that Kant does not attribute goodness to war; he limits himself to the aesthetic category of sublimity.[9]

But when he immediately goes on to refer to the opposite state of affairs, that is, to peace, he musters moral criteria, saying that a prolonged peace favours the predominance of a merely commercial spirit among human beings and engenders self-interest and cowardice. While cowardice can be taken as the opposite of the previously mentioned fortitude, self-interest and the general tendency to degrade the nation's character are *ab initio* to be classified as related to a moral evaluation. Thus the debasing results of peace are viewed ethically while the elevating character of war is viewed aesthetically.

This is Kant's position as far as aesthetic considerations go; the analytic of the sublime is a part of the critique of aesthetic judgment.

The second part of *Kritik der Urteilskraft*, the part concerned with the critique of teleological judgment, again refers to war, but the context is different and accordingly the conclusions arrived at are different too. Here Kant does not deal with the phenomenon of war but with the human motivation behind it. He refers to war as a thoughtless undertaking, stirred by unbridled passions. War is inevitable in the human context because of the obstacles rooted in human ambition, love of power, and avarice – all features especially characteristic of those who hold the reins of authority.[10]

---

[8] *Ibid.*, p. 89; p. 92.

[9] On sublimity consult the article mentioned before: Sublimity and Terror, *Idealistic Studies*.

[10] *Ibid.*, p. 301ff; II volume, p. 96.

Whereas Kant degraded the results of peace in the aesthetic context, in the teleological context he despises the motives of war. The moral evaluation emerges not only with regard to motivation, but also with regard to the results of war. Whatever the deep-seated stirring forces of war may be, war is a far-sighted attempt on the part of supreme wisdom to pave the way for a rule of law to govern the freedom of states. In spite of the low quality of its motives, the outcome of war can have moral stature, since wars or war may eventually unite states in a system established on a moral basis. Again, there is a discrepancy between war's immediate results which are terrible calamities and hardships, and war's ultimate outcome which is to bring about what Kant calls "culture." Culture is understood in the context of teleological considerations as: "The production in a rational being of an aptitude for any ends whatever of his own choosing, consequently of the aptitude of a being in his freedom."[11] This is a far-reaching statement, since culture is here related to freedom and freedom in Kant is both the pre-requisite for ethics and its objective. Insofar as culture is concerned, even in this rather extreme identification of culture and the cultivation of freedom, war promotes the highest development of the talents that minister to culture, thus creating at least the prerequisite for freedom, if not freedom as such. Broadly speaking, the evil powers visited upon us either by nature or by human egoism, call forth the energies of the soul and give men the strength and courage not to yield to the forces of evil. At the same time they quicken man's sense that in the depths of his nature there is an aptitude for higher ends.[12] The moral evaluation of war, therefore, clearly differs from its aesthetic evaluation. As a manifestation of evil, war is a dialectical pheno-menon *malgré soi*, since the results of war not only contradict its intention but prepare the ground for the higher ends of human endeavour. Whereas the aesthetic evaluation of war did not contain a reference to evil and whereas it was, paradoxically, peace which was seen from the point of view of its evil results, the results of war are or can be good. It is one of our tasks to show that the double-faced treatment of war in Kant's *Kritik der Urteilskraft* is not just a *bon mot* but is related to profound problems in Kant's conception of history. We now turn to the second part of our investigation.[13]

---

[11] *Ibid.*, p. 300; volume II, p. 94.

[12] *Ibid.*, p. 302ff; volume II, p. 96ff.

[13] War has been taken as an event or a series of events whose outcome could not be foreseen, – as Cicero had it, no one can tell the issue of war (quid futurum sit). *Letters to Attitus*, VII, 7, 7 (edited by E.O. Winstedt, vol. II, London, William Heineman, MCMXIII, p. 42–43). I owe this reference to my late friend Professor Ch. Wirschubski.

2

The issue which we are about to investigate is the coincidence between the course of nature or natural events and the moral idea of good, freedom, or the realization of higher ends, to use the wording of the *Kritik der Urteilskraft* again. The question can be more precisely formulated as the subjugation of nature to moral purposes. It seems necessary to distinguish in this context among three aspects or levels of harmonization between nature and the ethical realm, all three of which are significant for the delineation of the orbit of history in Kant's system.

Even when Kant refers to the concurrence or *concursus* between events in the world of nature or in the world of the senses and to the course leading to the realization of the moral idea, the distinction between the natural course of events and ethical aspirations must be preserved. Not to preserve it would amount to the pairing of disparate elements, which Kant warns against, quoting Virgil's Eclogue: *Grypes jungere equis* – griffins shall mate with mares.[14]

But in spite of the fact that this conjunction of different levels of events is not warranted, Kant makes a concession insofar as the moral or practical point of view is concerned. He does this when he refers to the divine *concursus* which is the divine interference or intervention in human affairs, traditionally known as providence. From the moral point of view it can thus be said that there is a divine hand which brings about a meeting of nature and of ethical goals. One way in which this meeting is expressed, is by the notion that God will compensate for our lack of justice, provided our intention was genuine. It is clear, Kant adds, that there is no warrant for the attempt to explain a good action, which is an event in the sensuous world, as a result of the divine *concursus*. When we try to explain a good action we are moving in the theoretical sphere; here the outcome of the Critique prohibits us from applying theoretical knowledge to the super-sensuous sphere. But what is prohibited from the theoretical vantage point is admitted, and even encouraged, from the practical and moral point of view.

It is here that Kant says explicitly that although we can very well explain the physico-mechanical cause of extraordinary occurrences, we must not overlook the teleological cause which brings them about in special ways. Among the extraordinary events mentioned in this context is the following chain of events: the wooded banks of rivers in temperate lands; and trees

---

[14] Perpetual Peace, transl. by Lewis White Beck, in *On History*, p. 107 note.

falling into rivers; and being carried along by the Gulf Stream.[15] If we introduce the teleological approach into our considerations, we can interpret the teleological explanation as an intimation of the wisdom of nature's foresight.

It is essential to realize that what Kant is saying here is related to the broader coordinates of his system, although it goes beyond them in some ways. In the first place, Kant is obviously referring to the basic notion of the primacy of practical or moral reason here: that which cannot be ascertained within the limits of theoretical reason, like divine intervention in the natural course of events for instance, can be assessed from the moral perspective. The notion of the primacy of practical reason in its systematic connotation has been confined to the ideas of freedom, to the immortality of the soul, and to God; yet in this context, i.e. the context of the harmonization between natural events, their beneficial impact on human action, and the realization of moral goals, the notion of the primacy of moral considerations becomes detailed. It ceases to be confined to the broad aspects of that continuation of reason beyond experience which is systematically and terminologically expressed in the concept of ideas and addresses itself to events or patterns of events.

The same applies, *mutatis mutandis*, to the exposition of teleological considerations. In *Kritik der Urteilskraft* Kant speaks of man as the ultimate end of creation upon earth. This position is vested in him because he is the one and only being able to form a conception of ends.[16] In so far as historical events are concerned, such as the wooded bank and the chain of events associated with it, teleology is again rather detailed. The teleological course of natural events has a purposive use for man from the point of view of his position in the sequence of historical events. These in turn are physical events, or else men's needs in his terrestrial existence.

3

The second level of action indicating a concurrence between events and human goals refers to human action or action in the stricter sense of the term, in contradiction to the level of events discussed previously, which was natural in character, although it served human purposes. Kant mentions several channels of human activity, most prominently trade and commerce, which bring about interaction between human beings and thus eventually some kind of community. What is even more significant is Kant's view:

[15] *Ibid.*, p. 107–108.
[16] *Kr.d.U.*, p. 294; II vol., p. 88.

though wars have driven men to live even in the most inhospitable regions of the world, this at the same time forces them into more or less lawful relations with each other.[17]

In so far as nature was concerned, a moral perspective entitled us to regard natural events as serving human goals. In so far as human actions are concerned, it can be said that, in spite of these actions, teleology serves purposes and moral ends either beyond the intention of the human beings – as is the case with trade serving the community and peace – in defiance of their intention, as is the case when peaceful conditions are brought about by wars. Of nature we could say that the whole idea of intention is theoretically speaking an imposition of moral standards on an a-moral chain of events; but in human actions, there is either a supremacy of one sort of intention over another sort of intention, as is the case between the intention to conduct commerce and the intention to create a human community, or one sort of intention overpowers another, as is the case when peace overcomes hostility. Here harmonization takes place within the sphere of intention, because of the weight of one level of intentions as against that of another.

Kant's systematic presentation can be seen as an articulation of the human popular wisdom expressed in the many proverbs of the most different cultural orbits. *Homo proponit sed deus disponit;* Man proposes, God disposes; *der Mensch denkt, Gott lenkt.* The reference to God in all three proverbs can be taken literally, as in Kant's harmonization between the natural course of events and divine concurrence; but it can also be taken metaphorically, that is to say, that intentions and results are not viewed to be identical or, to put it differently, that the result establishes itself independently of the intention. There is a Talmudic saying that whereas one might study the law not for its own sake but for an exterior purpose, one will eventually come to study it for the purpose of the law itself.

---

[17] *Perpetual Peace*, above edition, p. 108.

Already in one of his pre-critical writings: *Beobachtungen über das Gefühl des Schönen und Erhabenen* of 1764, Kant points to an occurrence or secret of nature which helps to shape a moral attitude. He refers there to "*Schamhaftigkeit*" (bashfulness) which, as a secret of nature, imposes limitations on the inclinations. Immanuel Kant, *Observation on the Feeling of the Beautiful and Sublime*, transl. by John T. Goldwart, Berkeley, Los Angeles, London, Univ. of California Press, 1973, p. 61.

Kant comes back to this issue in his educational reflections where he says that nature has endowed man with the feeling of shame so that self-betrayal may immediately follow upon lying, although he warns against overdoing things by constantly putting children to shame. (See '*Education,*' by Immanuel Kant, transl. by Annette Churton, Ann Arbor Paperbacks, The University of Michigan Press, 1960, p. 54 note). We follow the English translation. Compare: Friedrich Theodor Rink edition of Immanuel Kant, *Über Pädagogik*, in *Sämtliche Werke* 8. Band, edited by Karl Vorländer, Leipzig, Meiner, 1922, p. 191ff.

There is certainly an ambivalence in Kant as to the moral position of war, which occurs precisely when he uses a morally charged term like that of *Würde* or dignity. It is in this context that he says that military valour is held to have great worth in itself, and that war is often waged only in order to demonstrate valour. Since valour is a quality inherent in war, Kant goes further by referring to an inner dignity which he ascribes to war itself. It is because of this that some philosophers have praised war as an ennoblement of humanity. But, interestingly enough, precisely in this context where the moral quality of war is assessed, Kant refers to the Greek saying that: War is an evil inasmuch as it produces more wicked men than it eliminates. (The quotation also appears in *Religion der Vernunft*.[18]) The following would seem to be an adequate interpretation of the position stated here: Valour is somehow synonymous with the broad concept of sublimity, though it probably has a more limited connotation. In so far as we move from the aesthetic evaluation centered around the concept of sublimity to a moral evaluation centered around the concept of valour, we still appreciate the act as such, as the demonstration of a certain quality of fortitude. But insofar as there are long-range human consequences at stake, war is morally depreciated precisely because of its impact upon the character of human beings: because it produces wicked men. Here we encounter a view which indicates not only the difference between the deed before and after it takes place, but also the elevation of the result above the intention, with the good deed eventually carrying the day. Kant's general tendency is to show that this harmonization elevates nature morally or reflectively. He indicates results whose wisdom and goodness establish themselves over and beyond the explicit intentions of the doers.

4

But on the third level of Kant's deliberations, we find not only a mere discrepancy between intentions and results, but a clear-cut contradiction between them, since human evil eventually creates human goals. This is a far more extreme statement, since it means not only that trade created a human community, but also that the wickedness of human nature (*die Bösartigkeit der menschlichen Natur*) nakedly revealed in the uncontrolled relations between nations, eventually creates peace or a federation of na-

[18] *Perpetual Peace*, p. 116. S. Sambrusky has identified the source of that saying. See his note in: *Archiv für Geschichte der Philosophie*, 1977, p. 280.

tions.[19] According to this view, the mechanism of nature uses what Kant calls self-seeking inclinations (*selbstsüchtige Neigungen*) to establish the sovereignty of law and to promote and secure internal and external peace.[20]

Taking its departure from the wickedness and perversity of human nature, a condition is eventually created whereby man's moral disposition emerges and develops, until it brings about (direct) respect for the law by erecting a barrier (*Riegel*) against the outbreak of unlawful inclinations (*gesetzwidrige Neigungen*).[21] Kant sums up the discrepancy between the given datum of evil and the outcome of human action by saying: "Moral evil has the indiscernible property of being opposed to, and destructive of, its own purposes (especially in the relationship between evil men – *im Verhältnis gegen andere Gleichgesinnte*); thus it gives place to the moral principle of the good though only through a slow progress."[22] This is the statement which summarizes Kant's position on the contradiction between inclinations and ends, where evil inclinations are exposed to their own self-defeating results, that is to say to human good which can be achieved but only by slow progress. Thus we move from the practical supremacy of human ends over natural events to the conciliation of inclinations with a purpose and with moral purposes. Then we move further to the supremacy of the moral ends established by the self-defeating results of the evil in human nature and in the course of events it has brought about. This multi-level harmonization between nature and ethics, and also between good and evil, takes place in the sphere of history. Here the moral evaluation first presents a moral perspective applied to nature, and eventually leads to the attainment of the moral imperative by overcoming evil.

Yet in spite of the distinction among the three levels, it is necessary to point out that Kant – rather vaguely – uses the term nature to show that the good emerges victorious in the process of history. There are many instances

---

[19] *Perpetual Peace*, p. 99.
[20] *Ibid.*, p. 113.
[21] *Ibid.*, p. 123.
[22] *Ibid.*, p. 127.
Kant himself mentions one example of the empirical origin of a moral imperative in order to show that the moral imperative eventually becomes independent of its empirical origin. The Noachic ban on blood mentioned in the Book of Genesis IX, 4–6, seems originally to have been nothing more than a prohibition against hunting. It stems from a stage of human history in which hunting was the prevailing occupation. Its empirical point of departure was the fact that raw flesh must often have been eaten in hunting society. When this was forbidden, says Kant, so was hunting (*ibid.* 109 note). To use a terminology which is not to be found in Kant, one could say that the conditions for the formulation of a moral imperative lie in a societal situation, but that the grounding of the imperative is to be placed in pure reason or in practical reason just the same.

of this application of the concept of nature in spite of the fact that "nature" in the strict terminological sense is a concept related to empirical or theoretical knowledge. But that application cannot be held, unless it is used according to a very extreme interpretation of the concept of the primacy of practical reason, to encompass both the natural course of events and the ethical idea. Hence Kant says: Nature inexorably wills that the right should finally triumph.[23] It should be observed that Kant here maintains what he had said in 1784, in his "Idee zu einer allgemeinen Geschichte in weltbürgerlicher Absicht," that nature has willed that man should produce everything that goes beyond the mechanical ordering of his animal existence by himself.[24]

The optimistic or harmonizing component in Kant's analysis must be re-emphasized from yet another point of view. Not unlike Aristotle who said that evil destroys even itself, and becomes unbearable if it is complete,[25] Kant does not assume that good can create evil, but that evil may result in good. It is clear too that there is a fundamental difference between Kant's view and that expressed, for instance, in Schiller's well-known verse "*Das eben ist der Fluch der bösen Tat, dass sie fortzeugend immer Böses muss gebären*," which may be rendered in English as follows: It is precisely the curse of an evil deed that it must continually give birth to evil – a conception which probably predates Schiller. Kant certainly does not take the more radical view of assuming that a change in motivation eventually occurs, what 19th century philosophy called "*Motivverschiebung*," to turn evil motives into good ones. The evil motivation grounded in human wickedness remains evil, and a distinction is made between intentions and results. But this distinction virtually establishes history as a semi-independent realm which is neither immersed in the evil basic to human nature, nor elevated to the level of the moral idea.

Kant does not discuss the highest purpose of nature only from the point of view of human teleology or from that of moral considerations whose theoretical validity cannot be confirmed empirically (therefore it is called reflective only). It is said that nature demands that mankind should itself achieve the goal of a society commensurable with the greatest freedom; but it is also said that passions subsequently do the most good, since human beings are like trees in a forest: each needs the others, and whereas those living in isolated freedom put out branches at random and grow stunted, crooked and twisted, those growing with others must reach upward and

---

[23] *Ibid.*, p. 113.

[24] Idea for a Universal History from a Cosmopolitan Point of View, in *On History*, p. 13.

[25] *The Nicomachean Ethics of Aristotle*, 1126; Ross' transl., p. 97.

realize their beautiful, straight nature.[26] As was observed above, there are three levels in the broad connotation of the concept of nature. But in its more limited connotation it only refers to nature in the sense of a sum total of events guided by laws. It may be necessary to refer here to a distinction in a late short essay Kant published in 1794, "Das Ende aller Dinge," where he says in a footnote: "*Natural (formaliter)* means that which necessarily proceeds according to laws of a certain order, whatever order that may be, thus even the moral order (therefore, not always merely the physical). Opposed to it is the *non-natural (nicht natürliche)* which can either be the super-natural or the unnatural. The necessary issue from *natural causes (das Notwendige aus Naturursachen)* likewise should be presented as materially natural (physically necessary.")[27]

Taking advantage of the distinction Kant suggests, the following could be a way of summing up Kant's essential position: In so far as "nature" or "natural" refers to laws of a certain order, we may apply the term "nature" to the wisdom of the cosmos and to the non-physical or moral order of events. Thus the three levels of interrelation between events and their results are subsumed under the concept of nature and eventually history is subsumed under the heading of nature too. This becomes possible because history is the locus of harmonization and thus embraced by the broadest locus of harmony, i.e. nature. Insofar as we refer to natural causes, we refer to the events classified as belonging to the first level, that of causes and effects in physical time, linking natural phenomena like rivers and streams. When we apply moral evaluations to natural events, we eventually apply supernatural standards, and these are a sub-heading of the class of "non-natural."

We will now proceed to an analysis of the position of the constitution of the state and of political life in general viewed in the broad sphere of ethical evaluation.

5

Our investigation so far can be summed up by Kant's view that a meeting takes place in history between nature and the moral idea. We are about to explore the notion of history as a meeting-ground not only between nature and the moral idea, but also of different levels of human behaviour; thus history becomes the scene for the emergence of an area of human behaviour,

[26] *Perpetual Peace*, p. 61–67.
[27] The End of All Things, transl. by Robert E. Anchor, in *On History*, p. 76 note.

which can be summarized as a state's regime or constitution—*Staatsverfassung*.

Our first step takes us back to one of Kant's most renowned distinctions, that between legality and morality. Legality, as Kant understands the term, indicates a determination of the will which accords with the moral law; but the action it instigates does not occur for the sake of the law. Morality is an attitude in which the moral law itself is the incentive. Kant amplifies this distinction by saying that the distinction in an action which conforms to the law but is not performed for the sake of the law amounts to a distinction between that which is morally good in letter but not in spirit – spirit amounting here to the intention (– *Gesinnung*).[28]

But when we consider history, this clear-cut distinction between legality and morality cannot be maintained. When Kant speaks of progress, and asks what sequence progress can be expected to follow, he answers his question by saying that it is not the usual sequence proceeding *from the bottom upwards* but a sequence proceeding *from the top downwards*.[29] Why did Kant formulate his position in this way? The very notion of progress indicates advance towards the realization of some perfection or goodness. Perfection and goodness are ethical notions for Kant, and as such they cannot be deduced or even arrived at from the empirical course of events. The notion of goodness and its variations can be translated into history as continuous improvement,[30] but it cannot have an historical origin. A shortcut towards the realization of the moral good would make human progress already visible from afar,[31] and would amount to a total merger between the sequence of events in time and moral goodness as a standard and guiding idea. Because it is fundamentally or systematically impossible to achieve a total merger within the limits of experience, the only thing which can be envisaged and aimed at is a harmonization of the sphere of experience and the moral idea. Progress therefore amounts to human improvement and, more concretely, to the distinction suggested by Kant between two elements: 1) the *right* of every people to give itself whatever civil constitution it sees fit, without interference from other powers. And 2) the only intrinsically right and morally good constitution a people can have is one disposed to avoid wars of aggression. War of aggression, according to "*Zum ewigen Frieden*," is one in which the position, right and status of peoples are impaired; that is to say, it is a situation in which mutual recogni-

---

[28] *Kr.d.U.*, p. 84–85; p. 74–75.
[29] The Contest of Faculties, in Kant's *Political Writings*, edited with an introduction and notes by Hand Reiss, translated by H.B. Nesbitt, Cambridge University Press, 1970, p. 188.
[30] *Ibid.*, p. 177.
[31] *Ibid.*, p. 178.

tion is denied. If we look at the various formulations of the moral law, we find that wars of aggression contradict the principle of moral law in the most blatant way. The first formulation, according to which the maxim guiding in the direction of establishing universal law is defied by wars of aggression, since as a maxim of behaviour wars of aggression cannot establish a universal law. This is because wars of aggression presuppose a difference between the aggressor and the people attacked: in a situation in which everybody or every people is an aggressor, there can be no aggression. If we take Kant's formulation, which is grounded in the recognition of every human being as an end and not as a means, a recognition in turn grounded in respect for the humanity embodied in every human being, we realize that the moral law refers to respect for human beings, and that Kant uses the term "respect" (*Achtung*) both for man's attitude towards the law and for his interaction with his fellow-man. It can therefore be said that the avoidance of wars of aggression represents minimal human progress or the minimum realization of the various formulations of the moral law transposed to the sphere of history.

From the point of view of the factual basis of human nature, it can be said that although the idea of the progress stems "from the top," it contains a compromise with or concession to the limitations inherent in the empirical human condition. Human nature or behaviour exhibits a passion or enthusiasm directed exclusively toward the ideal,[32] but, empirically speaking, man's natural endowments consist of unknown proportions of good and evil. No-one can, therefore, tell what effect to expect from his own actions. The general improvement of mankind presupposes at least a limited will to innate and unvarying goodness,[33] – and this unvarying goodness cannot be credited to human beings. On the one hand, therefore, history is the locus of the least good, since the optimal good cannot be realized; on the other, total evil is rejected and, as we have seen, evil inclinations give birth to good deeds. There is thus a double optimism which is related to Kant's predilection for harmonization: the minimum of good can be realized and the maximum of evil defeats itself.

We can say that for Kant the civil constitution is a *tertium quid* between morality and history in the limited sense of a sequence of events, and that it is probably also a *tertium quid* between legality and morality. A clear-cut distinction between different sorts of motivation, or between the letter and the spirit of the law, can hardly be maintained, since a good constitution occupies a position in terms of both legality and morality, at least Kant attributes to it the status of being moraly good. We must therefore address

[32] *Ibid.*, p. 183.
[33] *Ibid.*, p. 181.

ourselves to the question of why the constitution is given this intermediate position. There is an affinity between the universality of the moral law and the status of the law. For instance, Kant expresses this affinity when he formulates what he calls – interestingly enough – the transcendental formula of public law: all actions relating to the right of other men are unjust if their maxim is not consistent with publicity (*Publizität*). Publicity can be taken as an empirical embodiment of universality, since it is an embodiment and continuation of universality, and provides for the openness of human beings to the law. Conversely a *ban* on publicity hinders a nation's progress, even with regard to the least of its claims, which is the claim for natural rights.[34]

Since Kant is referring here to the actual regime or to the constitution, the importance of republicanism comes to the fore. However, it is well known that republicanism in Kant does not necessarily mean a state without a monarch. It is essentially a state-structure based on the principle of the freedom of all members of society, on everyone's dependence upon a single common legislation, and ultimately, on the law of men's equality as citizens.[35] Republicanism maintains the freedom of the members of the society and their equality, whereas absolutism – its opposite – subjects citizens to the decision of someone above them who is not himself subject to the common legislation. It has to be observed, that the question of war is also related to the state's constitutional structure – negatively, since an *absolute* monarch is defined as one who can command that a war begin. War is significant here because it is a situation in which all state powers must be put at the disposal of the head of state. Asking the people whether or not there should be a war therefore becomes a *pars pro toto* situation both for the whole human condition and for the constitution. We saw previously that war is the minimal realization of mutuality; here it becomes an indication of the underlying principles of the state's constitution. Earlier, wars were an instance of inter-state relationships; here they are an expression of the state's internal structure.

Yet there are two additional aspects to Kant's view of the place of the state, the law and the constitution in the ethical realm. On the one hand, Kant views the legal system prevailing in a state as necessary *a priori* or as grounded in the idea prescribing what the principles of law and right should be. He uses the term "*norma*" in this context, translating it into German as "*Richtschnur*."[36] It is in this sense that the legal system or the constitution provides the objective or practical reality for principles grounded in reason.

---

[34] *Perpetual Peace*, p. 129; *Contest of Faculties*, p. 186.
[35] *Perpetual Peace*, p. 94.
[36] *Metaphysik d. S.*, p. 151–152.

But on the other hand, Kant indicates that, in their concrete situations, human beings are engaged in an antagonism which amounts to a confrontation of their respective freedoms. The practical reality of the state and the law provides common ground among different human beings. The state is thus placed in an intermediate position between the principles of reason and the acknowledgement of the concrete forces of promulgation which operate in the empirical human context. In any case, insofar as the state and the legal system are grounded in reason, it might be difficult to classify the state simply under legality as opposed to morality, since this classification would lead to the conclusion, that something can be grounded in reason without being prompted by reason.

Consonant with this rather nebulous position of the state and with that of history, there is a parallel distinction between the citoyen, citizen of the state (Staatsbürger) and the bourgeois, citizen of the city (Stadtbürger).[37] Yet, Kant also distinguishes between a good citizen (guter Bürger) and a morally good man (moralisch guter Mensch).[38] This distinction obviously implies that, in spite of the distinction between the bourgeois and the citoyen, the citoyen is not on the level of the good man. To put it positively, the citoyen occupies an intermediate position between the bourgeois, who is probably motivated by inclinations and egoistic urges, and the moral man who is fully inspired by the moral principle. This is most probably one of Kant's numerous attempts to bridge the dichotomies and distinctions in his theoretical philosophy, in his various deductions and in the concept of schematism, now encountered in his practical philosophy or in his philosophy of history too. The suggestion might therefore be warranted that Kant's distinction between culture and morality, which may not be consistent in Kant's various versions, belongs to the same context. Kant says that although we are cultured by virtue of art and science, this does not mean that we can consider that culture and what he calls civilization (social graces and decorum) make us moral. This is where he comes back to his emphasis on the morally good disposition. In this context this probably connotes the behaviour emerging from intention, whereas culture indicates an area shaped by achievements like art and science. The same applies to civilization where grace and taste are the guiding factors; these do not necessarily follow moral inspiration, or what Kant calls "Triebfeder" or incentive in the Critique of Practical Reason; Kant sometimes blurs the distinction between civilization and culture, referring to Civilisierung durch Kultur (civilizing through culture).[39]

[37] Über den Gemeinspruch, above edition, p. 92.
[38] Perpetual Peace, p. 112.
[39] Anthropologie, p. 255.

Yet Kant refers to the process by which man becomes perfected by pro-gressive culture.[40] In this context Kant is most likely thinking of human beings as determined by reason. Reason leads man to live in a society with other human beings and to undergo here a culturing, civilizing and moralizing process (*zu kultivieren, zu civilisieren und zu moralisieren*) through art and science. The explanation for bringing these three aspects of human activity together may lie in the fact that Kant views all three as human activities; human activity is juxtaposed to the animal urge to enjoy the lure of comfort and well-being, which is characteristic of happiness. Culture, civilization and moralization are listed together because all three represent an active struggle with the various obstacles presented by the brutishness in human nature. There is thus no way for humanity to achieve dignity except through activity, which can also be understood as the process of becoming educated.[41] Here again is Kant's ambivalence and hesitation about the locus of culture; it is distinguished from morality but still belongs to the same class as morality. We can therefore conclude that the different versions of historical institu-tions and historical activities of state or culture, indicate Kant's basic ambivalence about the systematic position of human-empirical activities and manifestations which cannot be subsumed under the heading of nature, but which can nevertheless not be elevated to the level morality. History is bring-ing the systematically differentiated orbits together; it becomes a *tertium quid* between the brutishness of nature and morality proper, and thus a locus of harmonization if not the locus for a fully-fledged synthesis. It might be appropriate to observe in this context that Johann Nikolas Tetens, in his "*Über die allgemeine spekulative Philosophie*," published in 1775 (with which Kant's familiarity cannot be doubted) stresses human perfectibility as the major feature of human nature. Tetens speaks of "*polizierte Völker*," in the context of the cultivated human understanding (*der kultivierte Menschen-verstand*), saying that the very presence of a regime (*police* or *Polizei*, eventually related to *polis* and to *politeia*) is a manifestation of developing human understanding and developing human culture.[42]

There is another component in Kant's evaluation of the relation of the state and morality, or of the citizen of the state and the good man, which suggests a different structure of relationship – not an intermediate position this time an interaction. A statement in the *Perpetual Peace* is relevant here.

[40] *Ibid.*, p. 253.

[41] *Ibid.*, p. 256.

[42] Johann Nikolas Tetens, *Über die allgemeine spekulative Philosophie, Philosophische Versuche über die menschliche Natur und ihre Entwicklung*, I.Band. Wilhelm Hebele, Reuther & Reinhard, Berlin, 1913, p. 512–513.

It must be observed first that in the same context in which Kant suggests the distinction between the good citizen and the morally good person, or sees the constitution established in spite of the conflict between private intentions and the common weal, he says: "A good constitution is not to be expected from morality, but, conversely, a good moral condition (*eine gute moralische Bildung*) of a people is to be expected only under a good constitution."[43] The question which apparently occupied Kant here was whether there can be a straightforward leap from the brutish natural state to morality, or whether empirically speaking human beings are already lodged in a societal and legal context. This context shapes patterns of behaviour and these patterns in turn have an impact on morality. States in their historical locus are, therefore, not only the mediators between nature and morality, but instruments for establishing morality, or to put it differently, they create the necessary ambiance for the progressive impact of morality. Man does not begin his self-shaping process out of nothing. Historical existence and its patterns are the empirical point of departure and they are congenial to the imperatives and principles of morality. Here again Kant is not suggesting an identity between *civitas* and morality; he sees them not only as belonging to the same realm but also as creating a situation in which *civitas* is the condition for the formative influence of morality.

We can now ask ourselves what led Kant to this new version of the interaction between the state and morality, and to his new evaluation of the position of history. We can anticipate our subsequent argument here by saying that whether, deliberately or not, Kant is making a concession to Aristotle's notion of habit or *hexis* here, it is because of an aspect of human progress which could bring about instability in the perpetual process. The following statement is instructive: "In point of fact, men, not without reason, feel the burden of their existence even though they themselves are the cause of it. The reason for this seems to me to lie in the fact that in the progress of the human race (*des menschlichen Geschlechts*) the cultivation of talents (*die Kultur der Talente*), art and taste (with their consequence, luxury – *Üppigkeit*) naturally precede the development of morality; and this situation is precisely the most burdensome and hazardous for morality, as well as for physical being, because needs increase much more vigorously than the means to satisfy them."[44] In *Kritik der Urteilskraft* too, institutions, states, their constitutions and legal systems, are instruments of stability and can thus have a regulatory impact on the infinite process and on the self-defeating devices

---

[43] *Perpetual Peace*, p. 112–113.
[44] The End of All Things, *On History*, p. 74–75.

inherent in it. Our reference to Aristotle sheds light on the systematical significance of these scattered remarks of Kant's.[45]

6

The word Kant uses to indicate the interaction between constitution and morality is *"Bildung," eine gute moralische Bildung*. It is plausible to assume, just from his use of the word, that Kant does not have in mind scattered acts of decision or even what he calls in his moral philosophy the causality of reason, but a prolonged or permanent situation. This is precisely what we find in Aristotle, first in his *"Categories"* and then in its moral application in his *"Ethics."* Aristotle distinguishes within the realm of quality between states and conditions; a state, he says, is more stable and lasts longer than a condition. One of Aristotle's illustrations is that of mastering a branch of knowledge: those who lack full mastery and are easily changed are not said to be in a state of knowledge, although they are, of course, in some condition either better or worse, with regard to that knowledge. Aristotle summarizes the difference between a state and a condition by saying that one is easily changed while the other lasts longer and is harder to change.[46] When Kant presented his amendment about the interrelation or mutual determination of a constitution and morality he probably had this aspect of stability in mind.

Kant's kinship to Aristotle becomes thematically more prominent when we consider Aristotle's application of the notions of state and habit. Aristotle says that anyone who listens intelligently to lectures about what is noble and just and about political science generally must have been brought up with good habits.[47] The point made here is that openness to moral problems

---

[45] The interaction between different aspects of human behaviour and activity is present in Kant's comments about education; he says that insight (*Einsicht*) depends on education, and education in turn depends on insight. In the area of education we may begin to free ourselves from circularity, because education is a process in which one generation transmits its store of experience and knowledge to the next. (*Education* by Immanuel Kant, transl. by Annette Churton, Ann Arbor Paperbacks. The University of Michigan Press, 1960, p. 11–12). We might suggest here that the state and the constitution are for political and moral behaviour what generations are in the sphere of education, that is to say, a given point of departure imbued with contents and characterized by shaping factors. The notion of *"Bildung"* occurs in Kant's reflections on education and will be explored presently.

[46] Aristotle's Categories, in *Aristotle's Categories and De Interpretatione*, translated with notes by J.L. Akrill, Oxford, Clarendon Press, 1963, 8B, 26, p. 24.

[47] *Nic. Ethics*, 1095; Ross' transl., p. 5.

presupposes a condition beyond brutishness, a condition already imbued with moral contents. These have already exhibited their formative impact by forming good habits. We may wonder whether Kant would follow Aristotle as far as his view of acquiring virtues by practising them,[48] but we can still make a distinction in the Aristotelian and Kantian sense between the moral virtue which is a quality of the character and moral exploration of philosophy. After all, even in his philosophy of ethics, Kant is very adamant about emphasizing that the ordinary human being knows the distinction between good and evil and possesses the proper criteria for evaluating deeds. Aristotle does say explicitly that moral virtue arises from habit and therefore indicates the etymological affinity between *ethiké* and *éthos*. Supposing that Kant had not followed Aristotle all the way on the statement that we become just by doing just acts, temperate by doing temperate acts, and brave by doing brave acts, – Kant would still have had to acknowledge the position taken in view of his various reflections on history, the political regime and constitution, namely that the situation created by a good constitution forms human behaviour and the human character and that it not only supports the "*moralische Bildung*" but is congenial to it. Here again Kant is close to Aristotle. When Aristotle indicates that the right training for virtue depends upon the right laws, adding that to live temperately and hardily is not pleasant to most people especially when they are young, he indicates that habit or *héxis* creates the most convenient point of departure for the moral education, precisely because, to put it in post-Aristotelian terms, good laws and the constitution embody the post-natural state of affairs and are already conditions shaped by principles. The pedagogical or therapeutical aspect is more prominent in Aristotle than in Kant, since Aristotle says that things fixed by law do not make situations painful when these have become customary. Moreover, Aristotle takes a more sober view of this point than Kant can, because of the latter's systematic concept of autonomy: Aristotle's sobriety is expressed in his statement "for most people obeying necessity rather than argument, and punishments rather than the sense of what is noble."[49] That Aristotelian statement sounds as if the constitution or habits are placed in the area of legality – to come back to Kant's terminology here. But it is apparent just the same that Kant comes back to the impact of *héxis*, laws and constitution in Aristotle precisely when he deals with what can be called the historical realization of the moral imperatives. Kant maintains that the legal system is not only an adjustment to human nature but also a necessary

---

[48] *Ibid.*, 1103; p. 28.
[49] *Ibid.*, 1180; p. 271.

concrete precondition for the impact of morality, that is to say, for morality to be the real incentive of human actions and decisions.[50]

This point can be summed up by saying that morality and human action do not completely converge in Kant. Human action is carried out by human beings; human beings belong to the two worlds, to nature and to the sphere of morality; and their own nature is not particularly benevolent and harmonious. Hence history is the scene of a *de facto* harmonization without it being assumed that the sphere of history will eventually be immersed in the sphere of reason.

We come back at this juncture to the question of the concurrence or *concursus* between nature and morality discussed previously, in order to place the subject in a broader context.

7

The fact that nature as it were plays into the hands of providence and moral ends has been noticed in Kant by commentators and described as an anticipation or adumbration of Hegel's well-known concept of the cunning of reason. (*Die List der Vernunft*.) It is therefore apposite to pay to this issue some attention, not only for the sake of tracing historical continuity, but mainly because it may shed some additional light on Kant's basic position.

Let us observe first that utopian thinking periodically takes advantage of this conceptual tool, showing that although we do not know the meaning of events, they nevertheless ultimately serve the optimal or prescribed end. Campanella's statement is an example of this view: "From this I realize that we do not know what we are doing but are the instruments of God. Those men seek new regions, led on by their desire for gold and riches; but God has a higher end in view. The sun attempts to burn up the earth, not to produce plants, men, etc., but God uses the struggle between it and them for the production of the latter things. Praise and glory to him!"[51] It is evident that in Campanella's presentation the two lines of action and events

---

[50] The meeting and discrepancy of virtues and morality on the one hand, and the impact of the political state on the other, has been expressed by Aristotle as follows: "... some people who do just acts are not necessarily just, i.e. those who do the acts ordained by the laws ... not for the sake of the acts themselves though, to be sure, they do what they should and all the things that the good man ought, so is it, it seems, that in order to be good one must be in a certain state when one does the several acts ..." (*Ibid.*, p. 155–156).

[51] Quoted from the translation of The City of the Sun or the Idea of a Republic, by Tommaso Campanella, by William J. Gilstrapy, in *An Anthology of Imaginary Societies. The Quest for Utopia*, by Glenn Negley and J. Max Patrick, Doubleday and Co., Garden City, New York, Anchor Books, 1962, p. 341.

follow the same pattern: human actions prompted by urges and natural events become subservient to a design prescribed by God or His providence.

Having observed, by way of an introduction, this pattern or let us say logic of utopian thinking, more detailed attention has to be given to Hegel's notion of the Cunning of Reason. The very fact that Hegel introduced the term "cunning" into his vocabulary is indicative of the underlying reasoning. It is not only that reason or concepts as manifestations of reason take advantage of the "natural course of events"; reason as it were induces natural agents to behave in a certain way and then reaps the harvest. This is inherent in the notion of cunning as a sort of lure or temptation to behave in a certain way. It is in this sense that Hegel speaks about cunning as might (*List, Macht*), as for instance in Zusatz to Paragraph 209 in the Encyclopaedie. Incidentally Hegel refers to God and Divine Providence here: the result is not the accomplishment of men as they are motivated by their particular passions and interest, but that of God who employs those seeking their own ends. Instead of indicating the *post factum* benefit gained from a certain course of events, there is a predetermined design which creates the course of events, although the agents involved are not aware of the design. Interestingly enough Hegel says[52] that the end posits itself in a mediated relation with the object. The end inserts (*einschiebt*) another object between itself and the object. Hegel regards this process of mediation, creating a distance by putting a different object in between, as the cunning of reason. It is clear in this context that what is elsewhere called "the total in-between" is the activity of the concept, and thus exhibits the concept's inner might. All these are indications of an a priori structure, so that the *a posteriori* (i.e. the natural course of events in one of Hegel's examples is the aggrandizement of a state or of a property), is instrumental. The harmony is there in the first place; although development of the awareness of harmony is a process which may take many detours; the process with all its whimsies, follows a design. Since Hegel himself refers to the notion of the cunning of reason in the context of a teleological outlook, and since he says that the true teleological outlook consists in viewing nature as free in its specific vitality – and this outlook is the highest one – we may sum up by using the Kantian distinction to say that Hegel holds a view of teleology which has constitutive validity – constitutive in the strict Kantian sense amounts to a principle which makes experience possible.

Kant says that it would be absurd to convert nature into an intelligent being and that the discernment of an intrinsic end of nature infinitely sur-

---

[52] *Die Wissenschaft der Logik*, II. Teil, ed. G. Lasson, Leipzig, Meiner, 1923, p. 477ff.

passes all our powers. "And as for such extrinsic adjustments of nature as are considered final (e.g., winds, rains, etc.), physics certainly studies their mechanism, but it is quite unable to exhibit their relation to ends so far as this relation purports to be a condition necessarily attaching to a cause. For this necessity in the nexus does not touch the constitution of things but turns wholly on the combination of our conceptions."[53] But what has been said with regard to nature at large also applies to human nature and human historical actions – and it is precisely in this context that we have to qualify the analogy which has been suggested between Kant's harmonization history and Hegel's cunning of reason.

Kant could not view the course of nature as initially congruous with human aspirations because he does not attribute finality to it. Man, as he says, is the ultimate end of creation upon earth because he is the only being upon earth that is able to form a conception of ends.[54] Hence the category of ends is a self-referential category in which man who conceives of an end is an end or applies this concept to himself. Nature is not the messenger as it were of a total reason, for nature is reason's externalization, and human passions are not an initial stage in the self-development of spirit. These elements which are so significant in Hegel's philosophy cannot be found in Kant because the dichotomy of nature and reason, or of nature and morality remains valid within the boundaries of Kant's system. Man can view the course of nature as playing into the hands of human objectives, or he can regard evil motivation as producing valuable acts – at most as a *post factum* congruence. This congruence is not a plan.

We can perhaps put this differently, by taking advantage of one of Kant's statements about the eternal peace. Nature guarantees for Kant even eternal peace through the mechanism of human inclinations. But nature does so with a security which is not sufficient to predict the future (*weissagen*) theoretically, but is sufficient to make it a duty from the practical point of view, or to prevent eternal peace from being turned into a chimeric (*chimaerisch*) end. Kant is attempting to present the harmonistic interpretation of nature and of human inclinations as a guarantee against imaginary ends, without being so incautious as to make it a foothold for the totalistic course of history, which is eventually an overriding synthesis of all the actual and potential components of the process in time. There is no way between theoretical dependence and practical justification to blur the boundaries between a prescribed course of events and the instrumentality of extra-moral and

[53] *Kr.d.U.*, p. 248; vol. II, p. 34.
[54] *Ibid.*, p. 295; p. 88.

a-moral processes, which benefit of humanity and bring about the material-
ization of the moral imperative.

An earlier essay of Kant presents a view opposed to the concept that there
is a *post factum* convergence of motivations which eventually provides ground
for the moral end. In this context Kant distinguished among men who
behave according to principle; the line of action may be extremely good
although the principles are wrong and the results of the action disadvan-
tageous. Another group of people acts out of goodhearted impulses. Many
people act this way although the fact that a person is motivated by these
inclinations cannot be considered to have any particular merit. The position
of these impulses is important since according to Kant they generally perform
nature's great purpose. This would mean that nature has a purpose and
utilizes different agencies. The third group of people has self-love and self-
interest as the great axis of its actions. The people are very advantageous
since their diligence, orderly behaviour and prudence support the whole.
They serve the common good without intending to do so. The evaluation of
the relationship of intentions and the results is interesting here: principles
may have bad results but self-love may produce good results.[55]

This brings us to the point made before about the detailed version of the
notion of the primacy of practical reason. The primacy of practical reason
does leave room for expectations which go beyond the limits of experience,
like the notion of the immortality of the soul, or God, – all notions, or ideas,
which transcend the limits of time and experience. The primacy of practical
reason permits a perspective on events from the point of view of moral ends,
but one which sees above and beyond time and experience, without blurring
the distinction between the theoretical and the moral perspective.

Indeed, there is a certain rhythm, both to Kant's theoretical system and to
his practical one. In the theoretical field Kant attempted to use various
systematic devices to soften the duality between form and data so as not to
make knowledge totally dependent upon what he called in his famous phrase
"a lucky chance" (*Glücklicher Zufall*). He also tried to move towards
systematization, while retaining the duality. The primacy of practical reason
which manifests pure reason has been regarded as the major systematic
device for establishing a rounded trans-empirical universe. But within his
practical philosophy Kant again faces nature and human action being
determined by natural causality, and thus poses the question of the realiza-

---

[55] See: Immanuel Kant, *Observations on the Feeling of the Beautiful and Sublime*,
translated by John T. Goldthwait, The University of California Press, Berkeley, Los
Angeles, London, 1960, p. 74. This essay (*Beobachtungen über das Gefühl des Schönen und
Erhabenen*) appeared in 1764.

tion *in concreto* of the moral imperative. He therefore seeks new connecting links between morality and data, parallel to those he sought in his theoretical philosophy. History emerges here as the locus for the meeting of existence and morality, with all the problems which go with it; Kant wanted to solve these problems by presenting a mitigated version of harmony and by avoiding a total merger of all lines of reality in a Hegelian absolute spirit. While trying to solve these problems, he reformulated them but quite possibly left them as they were underneath the formulation fundamentally unchanged.[56]

Our reservation about Kant's anticipation of the notion of the cunning of reason is grounded in the difference between Kant's and Hegel's systems. Let us quote the following statement from Kant's "Religion": "The rule of the good principle, insofar as men are able to work towards it, is, therefore, as much as we can understand, impossible of attainment otherwise than through the establishment and expansion of a society according to and for the sake of, laws of virtue, of a society which, to encompass the whole of mankind in its sphere is rendered through reason, the task and the duty."[57]

In contrast to this primacy of the social which in turn manifests the primacy of practical reason, Hegel lodged the self-consciousness of the identity of reason and the world, or made philosophy in its strict systematic sense a consummation of achievement. Hence for Hegel the category of identity served as a criterion of evaluation for every aspect of development, including historical development. Kant's philosophical position is an adjustment to time and nature which takes place in history. Though Kant looks at events and processes from the point of view of pure reason, he is critical of the possibility of suggesting an ultimate harmony between pure reason and development in time. Here again no complete harmony is established but only piecemeal harmonization.[58] Some of these piecemeal realizations will become prominent presently. We start with the personal dimension.

---

[56] The affinity between Kant's view of nature and providence and Hegel's cunning of reason has already been stressed by Willy Moog in *Kants Ansichten über Krieg und Frieden*, Falken-Verlag, Darmstadt, 1917, p. 15. The issue recurs in E. Weil's *Problèmes kantiens* (Vrin, Paris, 1963), as well as in the paper by Yirmiyahu Yovel, The Highest Good and History in Kant's Thought, *Archiv für Geschichte der Philosophie*, 54. Band, 1972, Heft 3, p. 238ff. If we use the analogy of cunning of reason in Kantian context at all, it seems that the analogy should be stated as a cunning of morals, where morals is parallel to reason; the expression "cunning of morals" is preferable to that of the cunning of nature, since in the Hegelian sense cunning refers not to the medium but to the agent. Nature and passions are media, whereas the agent is reason (Hegel) or morality (Kant).

[57] *Religion*, p. 86. The translation included in the text differs from that in the quoted translation.

[58] Consult the present author's: *From Substance to Subject, Studies in Hegel*, Martinus Nijhoff, The Hague, 1974.

CHAPTER FOUR

CHARACTER AND DUTY

1

One way of regarding Western philosophy of education is as merger of two concepts with different origins, which eventually coalesced. The first concept is *"Bildung"* which can roughly be translated as "formation" or "shaping." This concept has a religious origin, since *"Bild"* corresponds to *"imago,"* and *"Bildung"* derives from *"Einbildung"* which means "imprint" in the sense in which man's form is imprinted with the spirit of God, making man an image of God. The history of educational concepts is to some extent the secularization of the notion of *"Bildung"* to the point where it is no longer presupposed that formation imbues man with the spirit of God. Instead, as it becomes secularized, the concept also moves towards autonomy: man shapes himself according to his potential. The Greek notion of character is the second origin of the Western philosophy of education. Character denotes first the tool which engraves, and then that which is engraved (in German, das *Gepräge*). When the concept is transposed to the human sphere, character comes to connote the shape given to man's attitudes or the constant features of human behaviour. In this sense the notion of character could be said to be akin to the notion of *"Bildung,"* with *"Bildung"* referring mainly to the process, and character mainly to the objective or outcome.

Kant's scattered reflections on education are related to these two notions, though there are certain built-in problems in Kant's theory of education, if the term theory can be used in this context at all. These in turn are not separated from perplexities pertaining to his moral philosophy.

2

Let us start with the concept of character. Kant uses the term character first in a broad sense; he applies it not only to human beings but to efficient causes and says that every efficient cause must have a character. He understands the term "character" in this context as something stable or regular and thus as a law. He speaks of the law of its causality.[1] In this broad sense, character must be understood as a consistent mode of action or behaviour. But Kant immediately goes on to apply the notion of character to what he calls "subjects," namely to human beings and to suggest the well-known distinction between empirical character and intelligible character.

A subject which belongs to the sensible world has an empirical character. Because of his empirical character his actions are appearances involved in connections with other appearances in accordance with unvarying natural laws. Empirical character is therefore implicated in a single series in the order of nature. But the subject also has an intelligible character. Here the subject is indeed the cause of the actions which appear in the sensible realm but his actions are not themselves subject to sensible conditions.[2] In its intelligible character the same subject must be considered free from all sensible influences, and consequently from all determination through appearance. It is correct to say that the active being begins its effects in the sensible world *of itself*.[3] The distinction between the two characters leads Kant to the conclusion that freedom and nature can coexist in the same actions, if the actions are referred to their intelligible and to their sensible cause. Like everything else in nature, man must have an empirical character. But since man also knows himself by pure apperception, he is at the same time the transcendental cause of his empirical character. The coexistence of intelligible and empirical character does not imply that it is possible to explain why in any given circumstance intelligible character should produce just these appearances and this empirical character. Such an explanation is beyond the power of our reason.[4] In another context Kant speaks of empirical character as the sensible schema of intelligible character. Every action is the immediate effect of the intelligible character of pure reason, even though the process or emanation cannot be explained. No time sequence of "before" and "after" can be applied to intelligible character and to its efficacy in the empirical sphere of appearances.[5] The problematic aspect of Kant's concept of character and its educational consequences can already be seen in this oscillation about the coexistence of the two orders of character and in the impact of intelligible on empirical character.

In "*Anthropologie in pragmatischer Hinsicht*" Kant employs the term

---

[1] *Kr.d.r.V.*, B., p. 567; p. 468.
[2] *Ibid.*
[3] *Ibid.*, p. 569; p. 469.
[4] *Ibid.*, p. 585; p. 478.
[5] *Ibid.*, p. 581; p. 476.

character in both senses: a certain man, says Kant, has *this* or that physical character; but at the same time we refer to man as having *a* character in general, and in this sense the term character has a moral connotation. Character is in the first sense a criterion which distinguishes man as a sensuous being or as a being who belongs to nature while the second meaning of the term "character" refers to man as a being endowed with reason or freedom. A person who adheres to principles, whom we know to be guided not by instinct but by will, is a person with character (*"hat einen Character"*). In this more limited sense, character connotes a mode of thinking (*Denkungs-art*) and has the moral connotation of what man is prepared to make of himself (*was er ... sich selbst zu machen bereit ist*).[6]

We have already observed that, by implication, Kant combined the notion of character and the notion of *"Bildung"* which indicates the process of self-formation. Character refers to a "mode of thinking," and this mode of thinking implies permanence and stability; when therefore character is attributed to a person, that person is not only being described, he is being praised. Character in this sense is rare and evokes high respect, even ad-miration. This laudatory sense of the word goes beyond a *"Denkungsart"* and indicates a feature of will according to which the subject makes specific practical principles, which his reason prescribes for him, binding upon himself. Even though these principles may sometimes be false or faulty, man still possesses "the formal aspect of willing in general" (*das Formelle des Wollens überhaupt*), which leads him to act in accordance with permanent principles. Because this aspect of will and its formal features are present in it, character does not refer to nature's impact on man but to man's own actions, to what he makes of himself. A distinction is made between character and temperament, which generally indicates the passive aspect of the subject.[7]

In the *Anthropologie* (elsewhere too, but we prefer the exposition in the *Anthropologie* precisely because of the subject matter), Kant employs the term "sensible character" (*der sensible Character*) which clearly corresponds to the term "empirical character." But here he adds that sensible character must be viewed as naturally evil, while the inborn disposition of man's intelligible character is naturally good.[8] The link between intelligible char-acter and the view of mankind is to be found in an aspect of man's making or building of himself, which can be called "perfectioning himself" in the sense that man is capable of perfecting himself in accordance with the ends he sets himself (*sich nach seinen von ihm selbst genommenen Zwecken zu*

---

[6] *Anthropologie*, p. 205.
[7] *Ibid.*, p. 213.
[8] *Ibid.*, p. 286.

perfektionieren). Kant mentions several kinds of human activity in this context: he speaks of man maintaining himself and his kind, of his training,
teaching and educating himself for domestic society (*für die häusliche Gesellschaft erzieht*), and of his conducting himself as a systematic whole (*sich
regiert*).[9] We now have to explore the more limited concept of character,
which connotes man's moral quality.

3

Character, defined as a practical, consistent mode of thinking in accordance
with unalterable maxims,[10] immediately lends itself to a moral application.
It must be reiterated first that the self-formative nature of character prepares
the ground for this moral application, since self-formation, which is legislation of the self or autonomy, is the very substance of morality. In the
transposition of the broad notion of character to the moral sphere, a specific
emphasis is placed on the practical aspect proper and the term "maxims,"
which possesses a specific moral connotation, is frequently employed.
Maxims are the subjective correlate of practical principles in the sense that
practical principles are conditions whose validity is acknowledged by the
will of the subject.

When Kant speaks of a person as a character and translates this broad
description into a specifically moral language, he is referring to the highest
good in man and relates it to the moral disposition. The moral law is related
to character, and thus to the absolute spontaneity of freedom. It is possible
that the following conjunction is implied by Kant: Intelligible character is
related to the spontaneity of freedom. Since character is self-formation, the
essence of character and the essence of intelligibility coincide or converge.
It is in this sense that the character of a person and the moral value of the
person or his deeds are the focus of valuation.

The combination of self-formation and self-legislation explains why Kant
places the emphasis in his philosophy of education on what he calls the
formation of character, of which moral education consists.[11] Since morality
is a matter of character,[12] Kant applies the notion of maxims to the educational process or to its objective which is the formation of character and,

[9] *Ibid.*, p. 252–253.
[10] *Ibid.*, p. 174.
[11] I. Kant, *Education*, tr. by G.A. Churton, University of Michigan Press, Ann Arbor,
1960, p. 84.
[12] *Ibid.*, p. 96.

as we have seen, in the context of ethics maxims refer to the guiding rules of the subjective response to the principles of morality. Character consists of the readiness to act in accordance with "maxims" – which are subjective rules, proceeding from man's understanding.[13] Because of the conjunction between education, character and morality, a child must be made to do right not out of mere habit but because of his own "maxims." Moreover, super-imposing the notion that the incentive to action has to be the moral good itself on his philosophy of education Kant adds that it is the objective of education for a child to do right because it is right and not merely behaviour-istically.[14] Although Kant uses the term maxim in this context, this is precisely where he may be referring to the notion of ideas as explained in the *Critique of Pure Reason*:[15] "The *estimation* of morality, in regard to its purity and consequences, is effected in accordance with *ideas*, the *observance* of its laws in accordance with *maxims*."

Because of this emphasis on maxims or on inner conviction, Kant juxta-poses maxims and discipline: "Moral culture must be based upon "maxims," not upon discipline; the one prevents evil habits, the other trains the mind to think." Apparently Kant intended that principles should be internalized even if man has to keep the motto "*wie sag ich's meinem Kinde?*" in mind, for he emphasizes that a child should learn to act according to "maxims" whose reasonableness he can see for himself.[16]

With respect to the grounding of education in morality, Kant is anxious to point out that everything in education depends upon establishing correct principles and leading children to understand, accept and internalize them.[17] Since morality is the anchor of education, but education applies to concrete and empirical human beings, Kant is in a way facing the dilemma of the two characters: how does intelligible character affect empirical character, or else, how does character come to be formed? In a way, Kant was facing a problem here which is parallel to the central problem of his philosophy of knowledge – that of linking and establishing modes of mediation between forms and data. It is for this reason that Kant makes discipline the first step towards education and *a fortiori* towards morality even though as a matter of principle he sees a dichotomy between discipline and morality. Discipline makes animal nature human nature; the *tertium quid* between discipline and morality lies in overcoming of man's natural unruliness, for both discipline

---

[13] *Ibid.*, p. 84.
[14] *Ibid.*, p. 77.
[15] *Kr.d.r.V.*, B, p. 840; p. 60.
[16] *Education*, p. 83.
[17] *Education*, p. 108.

and morality make man subject to laws and rules or to maxims. "By discipline men are placed in subjection to the laws of mankind, and brought to feel their constraint."[18] Discipline is thus a connecting link between natural human life and morality, and its significance is that it can be imposed or introduced into the context of human behaviour early in life: ". . . Unruliness cannot be done away with, and a mistake in discipline can never be repaired."[19] "Men should therefore accustom themselves early to yield to the commands of reason, for if a man be allowed to follow his own will in his views, without opposition, a certain lawlessness will cling to him throughout his life."[20] Discipline is merely negative,[21] but it serves as the first chronological or biographical link in the chain leading to morality. Morality has no place in nature, for man's nature is neither morally good nor bad, and man only becomes a moral being when his reason has developed ideas of duty and law.[22] Discipline is behaviour which follows rules and it can thus eventually be developed or elevated to the level of morality.

The notion of discipline can be extended if Kant's use of the term in the Critique of Pure Reason is taken into account. Here, too, Kant distinguishes between discipline and culture, indicating that discipline is the compulsion which restrains the constant tendency to disobey rules, until this tendency is finally extirpated. It is interesting to note that Kant subsequently presents a very limited characterization of culture, asserting that culture is not intended to cancel any habitual mode of action already present but only to provide a certain kind of skill.[23] Kant introduces the distinction between discipline as training by constraint and teaching as instruction.[24] Hence the affinity between discipline and morality is grounded in the rules in both attitudes.

Yet this presents Kant with a dilemma. If discipline makes animal nature human nature and if all mankind's natural endowments must be developed little by little from within man himself by his own efforts,[25] discipline is human self-formation. It is not an activity of nature but a human activity. It might even be said that without it there would be no scale from discipline to morality. However, if this is so, self-formation is not only an essential feature of intelligible character but also a feature of empirical character.

[18] *Ibid.*, p. 2–3.
[19] *Ibid.*, p. 7.
[20] *Ibid.*, p. 4.
[21] *Ibid.*, p. 3.
[22] *Ibid.*, p. 108.
[23] *Kr.d.r.V.*, B, p. 737f; p. 574.
[24] *Ibid.*, footnote.
[25] *Education*, p. 2–3.

After all, education is about empirical man, and his development to the level of morality starts with characteristic human features. In this sense morality is the culmination of human self-formation, and intelligible character is the consummation of human deeds. But neither can be lodged on a level distinct not only from nature in the physical sense but also from the empirical existence of human beings.

A comment about the connection between Kant's reflections on education and his system at large is in order here. In a letter to Christian Heinrich Wolke of 4 August 1778, Kant criticizes the view that book-learning or schooling (*die Schulwissenschaft*) is the only necessary aspect of education; he believes that the essential thing is the formation of man according to his talents and character.[26] The juxtaposition of *Schulwissenschaft* and *Bildung* is clearly related to the well-known paragraph in the *Kritik der reinen Vernunft* (1780), where a distinction is made between the merely scholastic concept of philosophy concerned with the investigation of the systematic unity of science and the cosmic concept of philosophy concerned with the essential ends of human reason. Because of its concern with essential ends, moral philosophy is considered superior to all the other activities of reason.[27] Thus to sum up this part of our investigation, it can be said not only that education is anchored in morality, which in itself raises questions about education as the transition between discipline and morality, but also that the primary end of education is to cultivate the moral character. This is so because morality is the focus for this concern with human ends and is thus superior to discipline and education. The supremacy of moral considerations in the context of education reinforces the confusion about character's place in Kant's system. Character in the intelligible sense corresponds to morality, but becomes an objective of the empirical process of human development and "*Bildung*." Therefore, instead of keeping a dichotomy between the intelligible and the empirical orbits, Kant has to accommodate himself to the empirical level and find in it the seeds of the intelligible level. This will come to the fore in our subsequent investigation.

4

Once education is given a moral context, the concept of duty becomes central to the attempt to characterize the position and meaning of education.

[26] *Briefwechsel*, edited by Otto Schöndorfer, mit einer Einleitung von Rudolf Malter und Joachim Kopper, Felix Meiner Verlag, Hamburg, 1972, p. 178.
[27] *Kr.d.r.V.*, B, p. 866–868; p. 657–658.

84 CHARACTER AND DUTY

Let us recall that for Kant duty connotes what he calls obligation (*Nötigung*), or constraint, for he defines duty as nothing more than a *limitation* of the will within universal legislation. Duty thus falls within the broad concept of the discipline of reason discussed above, and is coterminous with submissiveness (*Unterwürfigkeit*).[28] A duty is a commandment gladly (*gerne*) obeyed is a contradiction in terms.[29] Moreover, because the definition of duty implies an imposing character, duty has reference to the empirical subject. This is why Kant comes to the rather extreme conclusion that the highest principles and fundamental concepts of morality do not have a place in transcendental philosophy even though they are *a priori* knowledge. Empirical concepts, like pleasure and pain, desires and inclinations, must necessarily appear in the construction of a system of pure morality because they are implied by the concept of duty. In relation to duty, they either represent a hindrance which we have to overcome or an allurement which must not be made into a motive.[30]

In the context of education or in the statement that it is a man's duty to improve himself, it is clear that duty is addressed to a child, to an empirical human being, whose duty it is to create himself, to cultivate his mind, or to develop his natural gifts, in order to attain the level of duty, where he is commanded to behave in a certain way, or to engage in self-legislation. There is the duty which has reference to man's nature, and there is the moral demand to develop and to obey the duty epitomized by moral maxims and moral laws and explored in ethical philosophy. To be sure, when Kant introduces the concept of duty in the educational framework, and does so in spite of the fact that this is not fully in harmony with his basic dichotomy of inclination and duty, he does not hesitate to justify duty by a pragmatic consideration: "And this will be of great use to them (sc. children) throughout their lives. For, in the paying of rates and taxes, in the work of the office, and in many other cases, we must be led not by inclination but by duty."[31] Here Kant realizes that the notion of duty has an affinity with the notion of discipline or obligation. He therefore shows the significance of the concept of duty in education by indicating that children must be subject to the laws of necessity, and that these laws must be kept constantly in view.[32]

Hence duty has a double meaning in the system. It calls on human beings to fulfill their destiny by emerging from their natural animal state, and it

---

[28] *Kr.d.p.V.*, p. 96; p. 85.
[29] *Ibid.*, p. 97; p. 86.
[30] *Kr.d.v.V. B.*, p. 28–29; p. 61.
[31] *Education*, p. 86–87.
[32] *Ibid.*, p. 85.

calls on them to become moral beings, which denotes a situation in which reason has specific ideas of duty and law. The first aspect of duty which makes room for the process of education is duty in the broad sense, while the second aspect of duty is duty in the strictly moral sense. We can still say that for Kant it is a duty, and a moral duty at that, to develop human nature, since such a development is a necessary condition for reaching the level of morality.

As a matter of fact, Kant is aware of the double meaning of duty, and even of the inner contradiction this implies, although he does not refer specifically to education in this context. He distinguishes between the ego imposing the duty and the ego doing the duty (*das verpflichtende Ich – das verpflichtete Ich*) and deduces both aspects from the meaning of the concept of duty. For the notion of being constrained contains a component of passive obligation, (*passive Nötigung*), and this passive component evokes the active constraint implied in the notion of constraining. The same subject therefore has two faces, expressed in Latin as *auctor obligationis* and *subjectum obligationis;* the obligation itself is called *terminus obligationis.*

Kant goes on to say that this antinomy or contradiction is only apparent. In his attempt to resolve the antinomy he takes advantage of the previously introduced distinction between the two characters, now referred to as the sensual and the rational being (*Sinnenwesen, Vernunftwesen*). He introduces the hybrid concept of a natural being endowed with a rational character (*vernünftiges Naturwesen*), in one of his attempts to overcome the initial dichotomy. Man is both the constraining man and the constrained man and this initial distinction between activity and passivity should not lead us to distinction between different substances, like that between body and soul.[33]

From the point of view of our attempt to show that education is one of the links between nature and morality, the conclusion suggested by Kant in the context of his metaphysics of virtues is significant. Duty's first principle relates to man himself; it is to live in accordance with nature (*nature convenienter vivere*). This principle has a more specific meaning which can be rendered as "preserve the perfection of your nature." This first commandment can be interpreted as relating to the status of human beings who are moving out of the natural animal state.[34] But, as we know from many of Kant's writings, "nature has willed that man should, by himself, produce everything that goes beyond the mechanical ordering of his animal existence, and that he should partake of no other happiness or perfection than that

---

[33] *Met. d. Sitt.*, p. 256.
[34] Universal History, *On History*, p. 13.

which he himself, independently of instinct, has created by his own reason."[35] The commandment to live according to nature paves the way for the commandment to go beyond nature, because nature has willed that man should live in a world created by his own reason. This could be put differently: "All natural capacities of a creature are destined to evolve completely to their natural end."[36] To live in accordance with reason or by human reason is thus the natural end of the evolution of man's natural capacities. By the same token the commandment that man should preserve the perfection of his nature, implies the self-transcendence of the boundaries of nature. Hence when Kant moves to his second principle: "Make yourself more perfect than mere nature created you" and in the Latin version: *perfice te ut finem*, we can only conclude that the state of greater perfection is due to the fundamental fact that man creates himself and does so already at the level of the perfection of his nature. We must therefore conclude that Kant attenuates the initial systematic dichotomy between nature and reason, or nature and morality, or at least that he makes several attempts to mitigate this clear-cut duality. Education is possible because the duality is not as stringent as it has been presented; education in turn brings the poles together since the development of man's natural capacity is the first step towards a response to duties and maxims. Hence, when Kant speaks of developing natural human endowments little by little, emphasizing that this development comes about by man's own efforts, he introduces a kind of gradualism not only into the process of education but into human scope in general. Thus, instead of a rift between nature and morality, a sort of gradualism is introduced through the backdoor.

This is even more evident when we consider the statement that it is difficult to estimate man's natural capabilities accurately. Some things are imparted to man by education, while others are only developed by education.[37] The difficulty here is to clearly delineate the process deriving from man himself from that deriving from exterior sources, perhaps including awareness of the moral law as such. The question is whether this is only a difficulty we are facing or whether it is a difficulty grounded in the absence of a clear-cut dichotomy between what is internal and what is external. The same applies to the statement referring to the proportional development of man's natural gifts to the fulfillment of man's destiny.[38] Here, too, the question is whether the development of natural gifts and the fulfillment of

[35] *Education*, p. 12.
[36] *Ibid.*, p. 2–3.
[37] *Ibid.*, p. 6.
[38] *Ibid.*, p. 9.

destiny are just two sides of the same coin, or whether the first refers to man's natural capabilities while the second refers to his moral core, which Kant calls destiny (*Bestimmung*). But if so, the two aspects of character, empirical and intelligible, re-emerge, and they can no longer be viewed as simply coexisting on different levels but become mutually intertwined. As a matter of fact, we come back to the double meaning of mankind's place in Kant's system here. No individual, says Kant, can ensure that pupils attain their destiny[39] since to succeed in this is not the work of a few individuals, but that of the whole human race. This statement presupposes the second thesis of the essay "Idea for a Universal History," where it is stated that the natural human capacities directed to the use of human reason are fully developed only in the race and not in the individual.[40] But for Kant the human race is not only the frame of reference for the realization of human capacities, but also an idea: human beings are very unholy, to be sure, but mankind must be holy to them. Mankind in one's own person evokes respect and its dignity has to be maintained and admired.[41] We refer to the humanity in each individual when we speak of human beings as ends in themselves, and not as mere means. As it is no longer clear where the boundary between human self-transcendence within the scope of nature and human self-transcendence beyond nature is to be set, from the point of view of duty and the educational process, so it is no longer clear where the line is to be drawn between mankind as a fact, a datum, or as the stage of human fulfillment, and mankind as an idea to be respected. One might venture to suggest that, since mankind as a datum transcends the scope of the individual, and since the individual is aware of mankind as a progressing locus for the realization of human aspirations, mankind becomes the focal point of human morality inasmuch as it is the historical or futurological object of human awareness. The descriptive and the normative aspects are no longer retained in their original positions. As these distinctions become blurred, so does the distinction between nature and morality. From one point of view, the process of education makes this blurring essential and at the same time the blurring makes room for the very possibility of education. We shall now see that Kant employs the different versions of the concept of duty to stress various directions in the educational process.

[39] *Ibid.*, p. 10.
[40] *On History*, p. 13.
[41] *Kr.d.p.V.*, p. 102; p. 90.

5

The extent to which Kant's philosophy of education is grounded in his ethical system can be clearly seen from the application of some of his major distinctions among duties to the field of education. The distinction suggested by Kant between man's duties towards himself and man's duties towards others is transposed to the child's duties towards himself and towards others. Let us look into what Kant says about children's duties and explicate from this the major issues of his ethical system. The principle which governs our duties towards ourselves, says Kant is to preserve the dignity of mankind.[42] This must be emphasized, since the concept of duty to oneself is grounded in the idea that human beings are representative of mankind and of its dignity – this is elaborated in the second part of the *Metaphysik der Sitten*. The negative concomitant of the notion of duty to mankind is that man reproaches himself for his evil deeds if he has the idea of mankind before him. This idea is the original with which he compares himself – here we could use a term introduced in the discussion about the relationship between intelligible and empirical character, by saying that man, comparing himself with the original idea, is a schema of the original idea, or else, as Kant says, its sensible schema.[43]

From the point of view of empirical human development, Kant is aware of the obvious fact that explicit awareness of the dignity of mankind cannot be possible for a child. He therefore suggests what he calls a catechism of right conduct. This would deal in popular form with everyday questions of right and wrong, for instance, payment of a debt, the awareness that another man is in sore need, and so forth.[44] The term catechism also appears as a note to paragraph 52 of the *Metaphysik der Sitten* [45] in the form of a dialogue between the teacher and the pupil. The principal notion explored in this dialogue is that of duty; it is emphasized that doing his duty is the universal and only condition which makes man worthy of happiness. Kant suggests the relationship here in his usual way by saying that we should not make ourselves unworthy of happiness by the dereliction of our duty, and that in this way we can also hope to be happy.

On the negative side, the emphasis placed on a child's duties towards himself leads Kant to juxtapose satisfying the child's cravings and inclinations

[42] *Ibid.*, p. 103.
[43] *Kr.d.r.V.*, B, p. 581; p. 476.
[44] *Education*, p. 103.
[45] *Met.d.S.*, p. 337ff.

with creating an awareness of the dignity which ennobles him above all other creatures. As practical advice on education, Kant points out that there are opportunities for making children conscious of the dignity of the humanity within them, with regard to uncleanliness for instance "which is at least unbecoming to mankind."[46] But the main point is that when he lies "a child degrades himself below the dignity of man ... Lying makes a man the object of common contempt, and is a means of robbing him of the respect for and trust in himself that every man should have."[47]

Here, in the educational context, Kant's ethical condemnation of lying is based on man's dignity, and not on the social impact or consequences of lying. The social consequences are to some extent present in the ethical works, when Kant says that lying cannot be a maxim because it cannot be made a universal law and that we cannot want to make it such a law, since the universalization of lying would make promises impossible. Though Kant does not explicitly argue here that lying makes social intercourse impossible, he comes back to this idea through the notion of the universal law and its application to the act of promising. But this is not Kant's only argument against lying. Lying is an intentionally untrue declaration addressed to another man (*vorsätzlich unwahre Deklaration gegen einen anderen Menschen.*)[48] Even though a lie is addressed to another man, Kant's additional and perhaps most central argument against lying is not the deception implied, but that lying is an indignity which deprives man of his character. Other men are the frame of reference, but Kant's condemnation of lying is justified by man's relation to himself. And indeed Kant says very forcefully that a man who does not believe what he says to another man is less worthy than he would be if he were a mere thing.[49] Thus lying is placed in the moral context through veracity and there is an affinity between veracity, honesty, sincerity and uprightness (*Ehrlichkeit, Redlichkeit, Aufrichtigkeit*).

In the educational context Kant combines the personal aspect of lying with its social aspect, underlining the fact that "lying presupposes the power of thinking and of committing one's thoughts to others."[50] The interpretation of this short statement could lead to the following nuance in Kant's thinking: The power of thinking is transpersonal, since thinking has an inherent structure and is not subject to the willfulness of any particular individual human being. By the same token the structure of thinking creates a common

---

[46] *Education*, p. 101–102.

[47] *Ibid.*, p. 102.

[48] Über ein vermeintliches Recht, aus Menschenliebe zu lügen, 1797, in *Sämtliche Werke*, ed. Vorländer, Vol. VI, Meiner, Leipzig, p. 202.

[49] *Met.d.S.*, p. 272.

[50] *Education*, p. 102.

ground and therefore communication among human beings. The misuse of thinking in lying is thus a contradiction of sorts for Kant. But since Kant emphasizes human dignity, he is bound to see human dignity not only in relation to man forming himself or obeying duties, but also in relation to man as a thinking being. The defiance of reciprocity is essentially the defiance of the momentum of thinking.

Kant in the context of the virtues discussed in the treatise on education also mentions humility. He defines humility as "nothing but comparing our own worth with the standard of moral perfection."[51] Elsewhere Kant defines humility similarly (*Demut – humilitas moralis*), as the consciousness of the paucity of one's own moral worth in comparison with the law.[52] In relation to education Kant warns against telling a child to compare his own worth with the worth of others, since this does not create humility but only excites envy. It is absurd to see humility in self-deprecation.[53] In the *Metaphysik der Sitten*, Kant makes the same point perhaps more poignantly, when he says that humility as self-deprecation in comparing oneself with other men is not a duty at all.[54] And *Metaphysik der Sitten* which is concerned with the elaboration of man's duties to himself, suggests a distinction between duty and servility (*Kriecherei*).

In accordance with his classification of duties Kant says that a child's duties towards others have to be grounded in his learning quite young to appreciate and respect the rights of others. This is illustrated by Kant's advice against telling a child who rudely pushes another poorer child not to hurt the child because the child is poor; the child's conduct should be criticized instead because pushing the other child is "against the rights of man."[55] To be sure Kant formulates his advice negatively and does not translate the concept of the rights of man to the particular educational situation. The analysis of man's virtues vis-à-vis other human beings contained in *Die Metaphysik der Sitten*, where love and benevolence are discussed at length is relevant here too. It should be noted that Kant also lists the duty of gratitude among the different virtues and defines it as reverence of a person because of the good that person has done us; Kant emphasizes that gratitude is a duty and not only a maxim of prudence (*Klugheitsmaxime*).[56] Since benevolence is central to the system of virtues, Kant stresses that duty is more important than feeling for the sorrows of others, and

[51] *Ibid.*, p. 105.
[52] *Met.d.S.*, p. 280.
[53] *Education*, p. 105.
[54] *Met.d.S.*, p. 280.
[55] *Education*, p. 102.
[56] *Met. d. S.* p. 305.

concludes with the statement that: "Children ought not to be full of feeling, but they should be full of the idea of duty."[57] Kant summarizes the lesson of human experience by saying that: "Many people indeed become hard-hearted, when once they were pitiful, because they have so often been deceived."[58] (*"da sie vorher mitleidige Wesen waren"*) or rather this should read: "when once they were compassionate." The important point is Kant's attempt to ground benevolence in duty and not in compassion. Kant uses the example of people who need compassion, and says that man's inequality is only the result of accidental circumstances – "If I possess wealth, to what do I owe it, but to the laying hold of circumstances favourable to me or to my predecessors?"[59] This indeed is one of the texts where Kant refers to equality not in the politico-legal sense but in the broader human sense.

6

As we have seen time and again, the educational situation gives rise to a confusion which is inherent in Kant's system because the educational process obviously refers to empirical human beings, while Kant is applying the various notions of his ethical theory which is grounded in pure reason and refers to *homo noumenon*. This confusion has another facet which can be seen by looking into the concept of virtue and virtues. While discussing human beings as free moral entities Kant describes duty as a compulsion of the self (*Selbstzwang*) which amounts to constraint by the moral law.[60] From the point of view of the concept of duty natural urges are only inhibitions in the mind of man to the performance of duty. In this sense virtue is described as a moral disposition in conflict;[61] conflict must be understood here as a conflict with natural urges and their impact on human beings. Virtues then amount to a meeting-ground between the empirical human being and *homo noumenon*, although the meeting comes about from above as it were, from the application of the concept of duty to a given human situation. Virtue consists in the courage to improve. Self-deprecation in the evaluation of one's own moral worth, compared to law, should produce an initiative to perfect oneself in accordance with the moral law rather than contempt for oneself.

[57] *Education*, p. 104.
[58] *Ibid.*
[59] *Ibid.*, p. 105.
[60] *Met.d.S.*, p. 211.
[61] *Kr.d.p.V.*, p. 99; p. 87.

But, Kant goes a step further in dealing with the empirical human situation, which has already been dealt with by implication in the definition of the concept of virtue. First, the decision implied in free self-compulsion has a parallel on the empirical level in habit. This habit is called the *virtue* of conforming to laws and such conformity is the empirical character of virtue (*virtus phaenomenon*). Its maxim is steadfast conduct which conforms to the law. This corresponds to the distinction in Kant's system between morality and legality, since legality consists in conforming to the law without making the law the incentive and motivation for conduct. From the point of view of virtue's empirical character, the origin or the incentives the will requires for virtuous conduct not even matter. And, even more important from the point of view of the process of education, virtue in this sense is achieved gradually, when a change of heart is not necessary but only a change in practices. In this empirical context Kant's example is that of an immoderate person who becomes restrained for the sake of his health, or that of a liar who becomes honest for the sake of his reputation. As opposed to this level of virtue, a really good man is one endowed with virtue in his intelligible character (*virtus noumenon*) so that no incentive is required other than the representation of duty. To achieve this level, a change of heart is required and this cannot be brought about by gradual *reformation*. It must be effected by a revolution in man's disposition.[62]

The question which naturally comes to mind here has reference to education again. It would be difficult to place education in the classification of a legalistic conduct and its guiding maxims for empirical virtues, because it cannot be assumed that an educated or educatable child adopts a maxim for the sake of ulterior considerations like health or reputation. Such considerations require prudence, and it cannot be assumed that children are prudent. Neither can it be assumed that the process of education in the meeting between educator and child will be guided by morality and the noumenal virtues, i.e. by the moral law as an indirect incentive of conduct. In terms of the distinction between the process of reformation and the process of revolution, it is easier to classify education as belonging to the process of reformation than as belonging to that of revolution, although

---

[62] See: *Religion*, p. 172 note, p. 42–43. In one of his earlier writings on education Kant distinguishes between reform and revolution. He says that the process of cultivation (*Ausbildung*) works against nature and that it would therefore be vain to expect mankind's salvation to result from gradual improvement of schools. What is needed then is not slow reform but rapid revolution. The context is Kant's interest in the pedagogical movement of J.B. Basedow, the founder of Philanthropinum in 1774. See: Aufsätze das Philanthropin betreffend, An das gemeine Wesen in *Immanuel Kants Werke*, ed. E. Cassirer, Band II, Bruno Cassirer Berlin, 1912, p. 465. The article referred to appeared in 1777.

Kant might suggest that the ultimate goal of education is to leap from reformation to revolution. Kant makes the preparation for "wise moderation"
an example of a process of education which has morality or character as its
objective. His guiding educational principle is the maxim "endure and
abstain" (*sustine et abstine*), and his first moral advice in the formation of a
good character is to put our passions aside. In the context of the theory of
virtues, this advice means that the obstacles or inhibitions to the process of
self-compulsion have to be overcome. Kant's more specific advice is to take
care that our desires and inclinations do not become passions, by learning
to do without the things that are denied us. This in turn calls for endurance:
we have to accustom ourselves to opposition or to the refusal of our re-
quest.[63] Hence the habit or custom already stressed in the context of the
theory of virtues becomes a kind of educational path to the awareness of
duty. This maxim is echoed by a second maxim *"festina lente"* which expresses both constant activity (*festina*) and a prolonged process (*lente*). Good
character eventually emerges as the outcome of this process of formation,
probably by some kind of revolution. Good character is marked by the
steadfast pursuit of the purpose and this is again expressed in a Latin maxim
"vir propositi tenax."[64] Kant eventually tries to introduce his basic systematic teaching about the relation between duties and the ends of pure practical
reason into his consideration of education. He observes that another man
can make me do something, but he cannot make me make what I am doing
an end for myself. That would be a contradiction, an act of freedom which
would not be free. But the combination of end and duty is not a contradiction, since to attain an end, I impose a compulsion on myself which
essentially coincides with freedom.[65]

Since Kant has to address himself to men's empirical conditions he has
to rely on customs and habits, – to come back to Aristotle's concept of habit
mentioned before. Kant distinguishes between different aspects of habit
(*habitus*). Habit is a facility to act classified under "readiness." Of course
within readiness, Kant distinguishes habit (*Angewohnheit – assuetudo*) which
is a frequently repeated action which has become a necessity of uniformity
from the readiness which is based on freedom – *habitus libertatis.*[66] Here
again we find Kant inclined to see a dichotomy between freedom and
acquired custom, because the latter amounts to a sort of necessity and thus
contradicts freedom. Yet, as we have seen, in spite of necessity, customs may

---

[63] *Education*, p. 97.
[64] *Ibid.*, p. 98–99.
[65] *Met.d.S.*, p. 213.
[66] *Met.d.S.*, p. 243.

lead to a good character. This is a concession Kant makes to the educational process, for it would otherwise be pointless and aimless. But even more important, without this concession Kant would have to cling to the initial dichotomy and to assume that a good character creates itself out of its own resources. The notion that man makes himself both on the empirical level and on the level of self-legislation in the strict moral sense is again a *tertium comparationis* between empirical and noumenal character.

The fact that Kant has chosen moderation for one of his examples of the impact of preparation on the formation of character is not merely fortuitous. Duty is a kind of restraint; it is therefore opposed to urges and passions. Kant takes exception to the Aristotelian notion of the mean: he interprets Aristotle as suggesting that the mean is a mean between vices. Thus according to his reading this would suggest that the difference between virtue and vice is a difference in degree. For Kant on the other hand the difference between virtue and vice is a difference in quality. Economizing is not therefore a mean between the vice of profligacy and the vice of stinginess. Economizing has a totally different principle from these vices, that is to say, the household's objective in economizing does not relate to the pleasure to be derived from property but only to the property itself.[67] The golden mean in Aristotle is indeed a kind of restraint, but Aristotle's justification was apparently not sufficient for Kant, since for Kant looking into excess and deficiency does not provide a principle which can establish the proper course of action. Kant probably did not pay enough attention to Aristotle's basic notion as expressed in the well-known distinction between virtue as a mean between two vices, but just the same an extreme to what is best and right: "But as there is no excess and deficiency of temperance and courage because what is intermediate is in essence an extreme, so too of the actions we have mentioned there is no mean nor any excess and deficiency, but however they are done they are wrong; for in general there is neither a mean of excess and deficiency nor excess and deficiency of a mean."[68] As is well known, temperance, which is moderation – *Mässigkeit* in Kant's terminology – is much analysed by Aristotle who contrasts temperance and self-indulgence: "... The child should live according to the direction of his tutor, ... the appetitive element should live according to rational principle. Hence the appetitive element in a temperate man should harmonize with the rational principle; for the noble is the mark at which both aim, and the temperate man craves for the things he ought, as he ought, and when he ought; and

---

[67] *Met.d.S.*, p. 239–240.
[68] *Nic. Ethics*, 1107; Ross' transl., p. 39–40.

this is what rational principle directs."[69] It can be said that Kant exaggerated his difference of opinion with Aristotle on this particular point.

7

It is clear by now that the duality of character and duty is one of the persistent themes in Kant's reflections on education. By the same token, this duality indicates that education is grounded in general considerations related to Kant's theory of ethics. We shall now see that two additional aspects of education can only be understood when viewed in the broader context of Kant's system.

Indeed, the problem is, as we have seen, "to give laws to freedom" and this problem differs from that of cultivating nature.[70] *Pari passu* with the distinction just mentioned between the laws of freedom and the cultivation of nature, Kant distinguishes between free culture and what he calls "scholastic culture." Kant speaks of pastimes or play as free culture, while scholastic culture is business (*ein Geschäft*). Freedom is manifest in games, play and pastimes, while restraint is manifest in work. Kant also gives preference to play precisely because it represents the basis of freedom, while suggesting as a general advice on education that it is free culture which must always be observed with a child. This distinction is amplified by the following juxtaposition: "In *work* the occupation is not pleasant in itself, but is undertaken for the sake of the end in view. In *games*, on the other hand, the occupation is pleasant in itself without having any other end in view."[71] This juxtaposition must be seen in the context of the distinctions and descriptions introduced in paragraph 43 of *Kritik der Urteilskraft* where Kant distinguishes between art and handicrafts. He says that the former is called free, while the latter may be called industrial art. We look at art as being free, as something which could only prove final or be a success as a play. A play in turn is described as an occupation which is agreeable in itself. Industrial art, being labour or business, is in itself drudgery and thus disagreeable. It is attractive only through its result, e.g. pay, and can consequently be "a compulsory imposition." At the end of all this Kant adds the following remark: "For not a few leaders of a newer school believe that the best way to promote a free art is to sweep away all restraint, and convert it from labour into mere

---

[69] *Ibid.*, 1119; p. 77–78.
[70] *Education*, p. 66.
[71] *Ibid.*, p. 68.

play."[72] One wonders whether Kant finds the suggestion of the newer school congenial, since his analysis of the free character of art includes the fact that even free arts contain a compulsory element which is called a mechanism. Without this mechanism, says Kant, the soul which must be free in art, and which alone gives the work of art life, would be bodiless and evanescent. As examples of the mechanical or imposed component in free art, Kant mentions correctness, wealth of language, prosody and meter in poetry.

A comparison of the far-reaching statement in the essay on education and the more sober and balanced statement in the *Kritik der Urteilskraft* shows again that to introduce the concept of freedom in the educational sphere creates some difficulty. Kant prefers play to work, and he places work within scholastic culture.[73] He obviously belittles the significance of book-learning for character as he did in the context of "*Schulwissenschaft.*" He prefers the maxim that children should be allowed to learn everything in play,[74] though he qualifies this maxim by saying that a child must also learn to work. He ultimately suggests that the two kinds of culture should be given different hours, and this separation by hours only exemplifies the basic trend of Kant's educational reflections which leads to separate play and work. But if this were so, Kant could virtually not connect the education of character with fulfillment of duty which is a mode of necessity or constraint. Because of this Kant is bound to be preoccupied with the question of introducing necessity into play and of restraining the inclination towards playfulness. In the *Kritik der Urteilskraft* Kant describes, phenomenologically as it were, the way in which play has its own rules and is not exempt from inherent restraints, and uses the metaphor of body and soul to convey this notion, as we have seen. In the field of education, Kant was swept away by the unequivocal dichotomy between play and work without realizing that this dichotomy calls for qualification in this context not only in order to go beyond the trivial suggestion about different hours, but more important in order to bring about the possibility of a meeting between character as formed by man himself and rules and duties as guides to this self-formation.

8

This last comment brings us to the impact of religion and religious notions on education. Let us start by referring to a somewhat optimistic statement

---

[72] *Kr.d.U.*, p. 60; p. 164.
[73] *Ibid.*
[74] *Education*, p. 67.

on the subject. Children, says Kant, will understand that there is a law of
duty without abstract ideas of duty. This law is not the same as ease, utility
or other such considerations. Kant even implies that children will understand
that it is something universal and makes this universality conceivable by
describing it as something which is not governed by human caprice.[75] The
reason for this optimistic statement probably lies in Kant's meticulous
attempt to prevent the idea of God from having any immediate impact on
the educational process or on the education of children. Because he does
not rely on children's "inner light" as an awareness of duty without understanding the theoretical idea of duty, Kant suggests to divert their attention to aspects of order to open their eyes and convince them of the existence of order. Order will then be understood in its ethical connotation
as duty or universality, or negatively as contradiction to caprice. Therefore,
Kant suggests that children be instructed about the order and beauty of the
works of nature and of the structure of the universe; from this basis instruction should gradually lead up to the notion of a supreme being as lawgiver. As a matter of fact, Kant may regret the fact that the culture in which
children grow up is so much imbued with the notion of God and his veneration that his own scheme of a gradual emergence of the relation to God is
practically impossible. He therefore says that "... according to the present
condition of society, ... we cannot prevent from bearing the name of God
and seeing tokens of man's devotion to him." On the other hand, Kant is
hesitant about deferring instruction about God until children are grown up
since postponement could lead either to indifference or to false ideas, among
which he mentions terror of God's power.[76]

The question which concerns Kant here is closely related to his analysis in
the last section of *Metaphysik der Sitten*, significantly entitled *"die Religions-
lehre als Lehre der Pflichten gegen Gott liegt ausserhalb der Grenzen der reinen
Moralphilosophie"* (The doctrine of religion as a doctrine of duties towards
God lies beyond the boundaries of the pure philosophy of morals).[77] Moral
education should be guided by the principle that there is no room for the
relationship to God in education where the rationale is provided by the
ethical system. Hence Kant says in *Metaphysik der Sitten* that (what he calls)
the material aspect of religion which concerns the sum total of duties towards
God does not emerge *a priori* from the universal legislating reason. It can
be known only empirically, and thus belongs to revealed religion and to its
duties *qua* divine commandments. But religion of this sort cannot form a

[75] *Education*, p. 110–111.
[76] *Ibid.*, p. 110.
[77] *Met.d.S.*, p. 344ff.

part of pure philosophical morality. We have to emphasize this point here by stating that religion is a doctrine of duties towards God.

The formal aspect of religion comes to the fore in its contrast with this material aspect of religion. That aspect can be concisely formulated as viewing all duties as (instar) divine commandment. Kant explains in this context that we cannot make the constraint or necessity of duty (Verpflichtung – moralische Nötigung) visible for ourselves (anschaulich) without assuming another entity and his will (einen anderen und dessen Willen), that is to say, God. But this duty which has regard to God is essentially man's duty towards himself. To perform services for another is not an objective obligation; it only has subjective validity for the sake of reinforcing the moral incentives within our own legislating reason.[78] To transpose this systematic exposition to the hints given in the reflections on education, we could say that it is difficult to maintain these distinctions between different orders of duties in the process of education even though, as a matter of principle, the whole aspect of duty towards God does not have a strictly moral significance. Thus it should not have educational validity for Kant who attempts to anchor education in a theory of ethics. Hence in the essay on education Kant concludes by saying that morality must come first, and theology after – and this is religion.[79] From a different point of view he says that divine law must at the same time be recognized as nature's law because divine law is not arbitrary and neither is nature's law, which is defined as universal and therefore as opposed to caprice and arbitrariness.

In his reflections on education, Kant is quite outspoken about the nature of religion and its human and educational significance. Since religion belongs to morality, it is a law in us, which derives its importance from a lawgiver and judge above us. Religion is morality applied to the knowledge of God. The only real way to please God is by becoming better men. Hence the many aspects of religion, like hymn-singing, prayers and church-going, should only give man fresh strength and courage to improve himself.[80] Kant even uses a metaphor which became popular through Marx, when he says that hymn-singing is opiate for the consciousness of people who praise God without thinking about how to fulfil divine law. For these people God is a pillow upon which to slumber quietly.[81]

We have seen that Kant assumes optimistically that children will understand that there is a law of duty, but children cannot comprehend all reli-

---

[78] Met.d.S., p. 346.
[79] Education, p. 112.
[80] Education, p. 111–112.
[81] Ibid., p. 113.

gious ideas. And here, too, the only educational advice for introducing children to the idea of honouring God consists in according with his will, and this is what we must teach children to do.[82] Through an explanation which combines the ideas of God and of duty, children learn to respect God's care for his creatures and their inclination towards destruction and cruelty is discouraged. When we come back to the previous analysis about the proper introduction of the notion of the supreme being in the educational process, it can be said that we must give children some ideas about the supreme being, but that ideas must be few in number and mainly negative: not doing certain things, either in overt behaviour like destruction and cruelty or in words, like not mentioning the name of God in vain.

We see that his discourse on education involved Kant in a series of systematic problems, all of which are related to the locus of education as such: education is a process referring, as we said before, to empirical human beings. Education in turn occurs between human beings, between society and the child, between parents and their children, or between teachers and their pupils. Education is the cultivation of abilities, but also the imparting of discipline. There are duties which children must be made aware of – and the question is whether the awareness of duties can evolve smoothly and naturally from the process of self-formation. We find that Kant tried to apply his basic systematic notions to the orbit of experience in the context of education. The perplexities involved in the realizing of ethical notions in the field of experience are reinforced by the dilemma Kant indicates – that culture is imbued with religious notions. These cannot be helped, but religious notions have to be placed in accordance with the systematic considerations: duty is the major systematic concept as far as self-legislation by reason is concerned.

Though the reflections on education are scattered they nevertheless exemplify, just as the writings on history do, the problems inherent in Kant's practical philosophy insofar as his philosophy attempts to be not only a theory of imperatives but also a theory about the actualization of imperatives. We are about to see another aspect of the problems arising in Kant's system when the concept of character is transposed from the individual to the collective or historical sphere. We will now deal with the notion of the character of peoples.

[82] *Ibid.*, p. 113–114.

CHAPTER FIVE

RACES AND PEOPLES

1

So far we have been considering history as the meeting ground between human inclinations and the moral idea. The material cause of history can be found in human urges and inclinations, but its final cause lies in the moral idea. We do, however, find another persistent theme in Kant – that of the collective entities – the races and peoples with specific characters, which manifest themselves in history and operate within it. This aspect of Kant's theory contains some significant problems which are not always explicitly discussed, much less satisfactorily resolved.

First, a preliminary remark about races. In his review of Herder, Kant notes that Herder does not accept the idea that the human species is divisible into races,[1] and attempts to take issue with him on this point. But Kant is torn between his desire to adopt a position which he calls "a transcendence of nature"[2] and his wish to provide an explanation for the distinctions and variety among human beings. He says himself that the philosopher has the option of admitting natural distinctions or of judging everything according to the principle "*tout comme chez nous*"[3] – "natural" needs to be underlined here in spite of Kant's idea of transcending nature. Kant was probably unable to find any explanation for the variegation of the human species other than that provided by race, although as we shall see, Kant's position is not without a certain ambiguity here.

In his early essay "*Von den verschiedenen Rassen der Menschen*" which appeared in 1775, Kant comments on the basic fact that all human beings belong to the same natural species as his point of departure for an exploration of the diversity among human races. This fact is validated by another – that human beings invariably reproduce among themselves in spite of their many physical differences in form. The capacity to reproduce is thus the

---

[1] See: *On History*, p. 47.
[2] *Ibid.*, p. 36.
[3] *Ibid.*, p. 47.

most important indication of the unity of a natural species.[4] The difference
between black people and white people does not therefore indicate that they
are different kinds of human beings, but only that they belong to different
races. This means that races are only varieties (*Varietäten*).[5] Kant suggests
an analogy with family traits (*Familienschlag*), and these are characteristics
deeply rooted in the reproductive capacity. When applied to collective
entities like peoples (*Völkerschaften*) they eventually create a permanent
trait or type (*einen dauerhaften Schlag*). The concept of race is applicable in
this sense; this would mean that the characteristic feature of collective
entities does not appear to be too insignificant.[6]

It is clear from this preliminary presentation that it is easier to conceive
and explain the negative aspects of race than its positive aspects. Negatively
speaking, Kant is attempting to contrast the concept of human race with a
presupposed notion of mankind's unity; that is to say, he does not assume
any basic primordial distinction between human beings and their collective
units or groups. But he does appear to wonder how the emergence of typical
varieties can be explained. Typical varieties become permanent entities
through reproduction. But reproduction absorbs in itself the limitations and
divisions implied in typical features and ongoing traits. It is evident that the
initial leap from unity to variety remains unexplained, even if variety is given
a secondary significance.

Kant makes several scattered observations about nature's impact on
human diversity. For instance, the air and the sun seem to be the factors with
the most significant impact on the reproductive capacity, bringing about a
permanent transformation or evolution of the seeds and dispositions as hereditary factors (*Keime und Anlagen*) which form races. The most significant
factor from the point of view of the reproductive capacity is not the main-
tenance of life, but its origin (*Erhaltungsquelle*).[7]

Man's interaction with his natural environment is illustrated by what
happens when man is transposed to the ice zone. This had – *musste* – (in the
course of time) to result in a diminution of the physical stature of the people
occupying that zone. The explanation for this lies in the interrelationship
of blood circulation and the heart: when the power of the heart or the heartbeat remains the same, blood circulates more quickly; pulsation or the
heartbeat is therefore accelerated and the heat of the blood increases. The

---

[4] Von den verschiedenen Rassen der Menschen, *Immanuel Kants Werke*, ed. E. Cassirer,
Band II, Berlin, Bruno Cassirer, 1912, p. 445.

[5] *Ibid.*, p. 446–447.

[6] *Ibid.*, p. 447.

[7] *Ibid.*, p. 452.

fact that smaller physical stature is more suited to the environment eventually has an impact on the development of the descendents of the inhabitants of the ice zone. A similar environmental explanation is advanced to explain the effects of damp heat (*feuchte Hitze*) on the development of human beings. There are other scattered remarks in Kant about the impact of environment on human development. But Kant is not completely satisfied with what he calls the "description of nature." Description does not supply a sufficient cause (*Grund*) or satisfactory explanation for the manifold human variations. What is required, he says, is a history of nature (*eine Geschichte der Natur*) – a somewhat daring enterprise for Kant since no such history as yet existed.[8] This projected venture into science would probably belong to the discipline of anthropology.[9]

Both from the point of view of Kant's later development and from that of the systematic problems relating to Kant's conception of history, we are bound to ask some questions about the interdependence of natural factors and the historical factors involved in human activities, in inter-human relations and in the relations between generations. One might argue that Kant's early essay did not address itself to these systematic issues because the system had not yet been conceived. But a later essay, "*Bestimmung des Begriffs einer Menschenrasse*" written in 1785, proves no more illuminating with respect to the interrelationship between the different components of history. In this essay skin colour becomes the principal external sign of human groups, now called *Stämme* or tribes. Tribes are not original; nature gave each tribe the characteristics it required for adaptation to the climate in which it lived.[10] Here too Kant maintains his earlier distinction between features pertaining to the human species and those which only pertain to race. Whatever is to be attributed to the species, and thus is a common feature of all men, is inescapably hereditary (*unausbleiblich erblich*). Human races are therefore different classes (*Klassenunterschied*) of one and the same tribe.[11] The inheritability of features, what Kant calls *Anarten* in this essay, is what is characteristic of the human race. The only explanation Kant offers for the transition from the unity of mankind to the diversity of races is the requirement of climate (*Bedürfnis des Klimas*). Our point of departure is the existing variety of human tribes or classes, and we cannot conjecture about what the first human tribe may have been like.[12]

The only thing to be said for Kant's later exploration of face is that he

---

[8] *Ibid.*, p. 459.
[9] *Ibid.*, 469.
[10] Bestimmung des Begriffs einer Menschenrasse, 1785, *I. Kant Sämtliche Werke*, Achter Band, ed. Karl Vorländer, Leipzig, Felix Meiner, 1922, p. 119.
[11] *Ibid.*, p. 120–121.
[12] *Ibid.*, p. 127.

deliberately uses a biological model of heredity to explain the persistence of limited divisions or differences in mankind. But once again, he cannot explain the interaction between human deeds and the impact of nature. The concept of mankind's basic unity, which has both a biological and a moral meaning, is central to both the earlier and the later exploration of the concept of race. This is why Kant is so adamant about making races secondary developments, which he calls *Abartung*, and by the Latin term *progenies classificae*, a term which reappears in a late essay "*Über den Gebrauch teleologischer Prinzipien in der Philosophie*" (1788).[13] Kant's reliance on nature in all these discussions or, to put it negatively, the fact that he refrains from going into immanent historical causes is telling. He says, for instance, that nature seems to be preventing a fusion (*Zusammenschmelzung*) of races because fusion would run counter to nature's end which is variety of characters.[14]

A terminological comment is apposite at this point. Kant uses the term "character" or "characters" to describe the various collective human units even though his frame of reference is the biological sum-total of features displayed by human entities. He does not question the applicability of a concept which has the specific meaning of self-formation in his moral, educational and anthropological reflections to the sphere of man's relationship with his natural environment. The term "character" used in connection with collective human entities, to describe the souls of peoples, is a Kantian variation on the theme of *Volksgeist* or *Volksseele*.[15] It is interesting to note that both in his critical period and later, Kant applies the notion of *Volkscharacter* quite widely. We therefore turn to the investigation of this concept and its bearing upon the assessment of the historical orbit.

2

The concept of national character appears in Kant's early writings as well as in his Anthropology. He mentions Hume's analysis of national character in both periods – in the first by referring to a detail about the intellectual capacity of Negroes, and in the second by recalling Hume's comment that

---

[13] Über den Gebrauch teleologischer Prinzipien in der Philosophie, 1788, in *I. Kant Sämtliche Werke*, Achter Band, ed. Karl Vorländer, Leipzig, Felix Meiner Verlag, p. 136.

[14] *Ibid.*, p. 130.

[15] The concept of the character of peoples is obviously related to the notion of *Volksgeist* and its transformations. See this author's article: Volksgeist, in *Dictionary of the History of Ideas, Studies of Selective Pivotal Ideas*, ed. Philip Wiener, IV, New York, 1973, p. 490ff.

each individual in a nation may have a character but that the nation as such does not possess a character. Kant takes exception to this, saying: "The character affected is precisely the general character of a people to which he himself (i.e. Hume) belonged."[16] "Affecting" here is to be understood as a continuous mental habit which would be rendered in German as *Gemüts-bewegung*. Among the traits mentioned are proud rudeness as opposed to polite approachability.

Before proceeding to a more detailed analysis of Kant's position and of the problems related to it, let us consider some aspects of Hume's description of national character. On what grounds did Kant assume that Hume denies the existence of national characters and confines his analysis to individuals? In his essay entitled "Of National Characters," Hume says that a nation is nothing but a collection of individuals. But, he adds, the national character is visible all the same, and the manners of individuals are frequently determined by the same causes which determine the nations's character. He also speaks of traits like gaiety and wit as characteristic of the French, or knowledge as characteristic of the English, or honesty as characteristic of the Swiss, although he emphasizes that there are exceptions and that all individuals should not be included under the same censure.[17]

But the thing to be stressed in Hume is his analysis of the causes which give rise to national characters. He distinguishes between moral and physical causes. Moral causes are those circumstances which work on the mind as *motifs* or reasons, and make a peculiar set of manner habitual. Among these are the nature of government, revolutions in public affairs, the plenty or penury in which the people lives, and the nation's relationship with its neighbours. The moral causes are therefore in fact historical ones. The physical causes Hume lists include qualities of air and climate which are supposed to work insensibly on the temper, altering the tone and habits of the body and giving it a particular complexion. Kant mentions the mode of government and climate and soil in his Anthropology, but he points out that to stress the form of government is to leave the question of the origin of that form unexplained, since it cannot be explained from climate and soil. He mentions the fact that the migrations of peoples have shown that they do not change their character in their new location.[18] He even speaks of the inborn character, of which the acquired artificial character is only a result. The obvious question to be asked here is how can character be inborn, or,

[16] *Anthropologie*, p. 239.
[17] Of national characters, in *Essays*, by David Hume, London, Routledge and Kegan Paul Ltd., New York, Dutton & Co., p. 144.
[18] *Anthropologie*, p. 2441.

alternatively, how can Kant maintain the distinction between what is inborn and what is acquired if "character" refers to man's self-made essence?
If we use the dichotomy of inborn and artificial at all, "character" has to be
classified as something artificial in the first place. All that Kant could say
was that there is no explanation for the emergence of character and that the
distinction between the two kinds of causes provides no explanation. As a
matter of fact, what Kant says in an earlier statement is more mitigated
than the statement: Whether these national differences are contingent and
dependent upon the times and the type of government or are bound by a
certain necessity to the climate, I do not here enquire.[19] It may be that in the
Observations on the Beautiful and Sublime Kant is less concerned with the
causes responsible for the emergence of national character than with the
expression of character. He says that a people's mental character (*die Ge-
mütscharactere der Völkerschaften*) is most discernible in its morality. It is
from this point of view that Kant refers the distinction between the beautiful
and the sublime to manifestations of character. There is, however, no explanation as to how characters come to be expressed in these two different
manifestations, or as to what makes these the most appropriate expressions,
or as to how these expressions in turn become factors shaping the constancy
of character. When Kant says that there is no explanation for the types of
government which are allegedly responsible for types of people, he can go
on to question what makes a given expression the expression of one people
rather than another.

In another essay, Hume makes delicacy and passion criteria by means of
which people can be distinguished. He speaks of people, not of peoples, but
is aware of the similarities and differences between delicacy of taste and
delicacy of passion. Delicacy of passion makes people sensitive to the accidents of life, while delicacy of taste makes them sensitive to art and renders
them capable of judicious conversation. Hume prefers delicacy of taste to
delicacy of passion, because it favours love and friendship.[20] Kant makes
the distinction between the beautiful and the sublime his point of departure
in characterizing different types of people, the sexes and collective entities
like peoples. Night is sublime, day is beautiful. The sublime moves, while
the beautiful charms. Understanding is sublime and beautiful. Courage is
great and sublime, artfulness (*List*) low but beautiful. Veracity and honesty
are simple and noble; just and pleasant flattery are delicate and beautiful.
Of the moral attributes, Kant says that true virtue alone is sublime. This

---

[19] *Observations on the Feeling of the Beautiful and Sublime*, tr. John T. Goldthwait,
Los Angeles, University of California Press, 1973, p. 97 note.
[20] Of the Delicacy of Taste and Passion, *ibid.*, p. 1ff.

would suggest that sublimity, which has reference to moral attributes and true virtue, should be most highly valued, but it is doubtful if Kant takes here an evaluative position. When he applies the distinction between the predisposition to the beautiful and the predisposition to the sublime, he says that the French and the Italians have a feeling for the beautiful while the Germans, the English and the Spanish have a feeling for the sublime. And even though he makes sublimity a teacher of moral virtue, Kant says of his own age that it is characterized by a sound taste for the beautiful and the novel which blossoms in the arts, in the sciences and in the sphere of morals.[21]

But the inner historical factors which bring about what Kant calls the palingenesis of features remain obscure. We are left in the dark about the significance of this propensity of peoples to pursue the beautiful rather than the sublime or vice versa, just as Hume's account leaves us in the dark about why individuals have a propensity either for taste or for passion. It is a lucky accident that some peoples have been influenced by one, some by the other. And there are even differences among peoples between the French and the Italians or the English and the Spanish. History has become a meeting ground not only for races as sub-types of the human species with characteristic features but also for peoples as historical entities and their various sensitivities to ideational influences. Nor does the Anthropology offer an explanation for the character of peoples, even though it does deal with this, together with the character of sexes, races and mankind at large.

3

Die Anthropologie in pragmatischer Hinsicht (1788) does show that the character of a people (*populus*) is related to its existence. Kant defines "people" as a mass of human beings inhabiting a common strip of land and forming a whole (*ein Ganzes*). He then distinguishes between nation (*gens*) and mob (*vulgus*). A nation (from the root *nascere*) is a mass of people or part of a people united by common descent and forming a civil totality (*ein bürgerliches Ganzes*),[22] while a mob is a part of a people which excludes itself from the laws of the civil totality it is a wild mass within the people.

This description of "nation" is rather curious. It combines the notion of common descent, which suggests the concept of race analyzed above, with the concept of civil society, which is central – as we have seen – to Kant's

---

[21] *Observations on the Feeling*, p. 47, 51, 57, 97, 115.
[22] *Anthropologie*, p. 239.

theory of history, of politics and the state. Kant does not show the extent to which these two factors, descent and state organization, either coincide in fact or coincide by virtue of the inner logic of human activities. If the end is a universal civil society, as the Fifth Thesis of the Idea for a Universal History from a Cosmopolitan Point of View would have it, one might also ask whether nature's broad design for a universal society is consonant with a civil society bounded by common descent.

Be that as it may, Kant's definition of "people" combines the natural factor of descent with the organizational factor of civil society without explaining the reason for that synthesis. The same occurs when Kant discusses the emergence of a people's character. Is this character due to natural descent or to political civil society, or is it to be placed between the two which would make it co-extensive with the concept "people?" Kant uses this concept pragmatically, to indicate the free conduct of human beings who are led to fulfill objectives advocated by the senses;[23] from this point of view it is the manifestation of certain traits which is important, rather than their origin.[24] Kant goes on to list peoples and their traits in terms of vitality, the taste for conversation, the spirit of freedom, the spirit of trade, solemnity (*Feierlichkeit*), gaiety, steadfastness et al. The statement that even a systematic theory of human behaviour does not call for an analysis of the origin of its *Gestalt* relieves Kant of the necessity of placing stable entities of collective character in history. It also exempts him from explaining the stability of human behaviour, for it is a major tenet of Kant's ethical theory that human behaviour does not obey automatically the laws of reason. If reason annihilates accidents, as Wilhelm von Humboldt has it, reason is not realized by historical agents and their activity, in spite of the centrality of reason in Kant's ethical theory.

In fact it is necessary to broaden the scope of the problems inherent in Kant's description and analysis of the actual historical process. The very importance of Kant's anthropological reflections has been belittled, but this approach does not do justice to the fact that some of the major issues in Kant's system reemerge in his anthropological studies – such as problems related to the capacity of knowing, to satisfaction and dissatisfaction, and, more important, to the concept of character which is central to the analysis of the anthropological situation. We have seen that the notion of human races is not accidental in Kant, but appears in both his early and his late writings. Moreover, the concept of the character of peoples is an attempt to reinterpret the notion of human races. In view of all this, a confrontation of

[23] *Kr.d.r.V.*, B, 828; 632.
[24] *Anthropologie*, p. 240.

Kant's historical observations with his broad theory of practice is inescapable. Some aspects of this confrontation have already appeared in Kant's political theory and in his reflections on education. The persistent reappearance in Kant's anthropological investigation of the same problems only confirms the fact that the real question at issue is the encounter between human needs and the moral imperative. It is interesting to note that in his study of human races and groupings, Kant does not raise the question of the relationship between the actual course of events which relate to collective entities and the notion of progress. He does not even raise the question of the relationship between individuals and peoples, if we assume that the imperatives of practical reason devolve upon individuals and not collectives, because only individuals can be motivated by reason. Of course, groups have a sort of subliminal intentionality towards certain notions and ideas inasmuch as groups of individuals have a certain attitude towards beauty or sublimity. But Kant does not ask whether they have this sort of intentionality towards the moral law and its maxims. Is this omission accidental, or does it relate to the systematic issue which concerns us here: there are day-to-day-acts and there is action inspired by the moral law – how do they come together, or are they separated by an unbridgeable chasm? The inner logic of Kant's system is such that this remains an open question.[25]

4

In his essay entitled "The conjectural beginning of human history" (*Mutmasslicher Anfang der Menschengeschichte*, 1786), Kant says explicitly that we must start out with something which human reason cannot derive from prior natural causes, namely the existence of man.[26] If this is to be taken literally and systematically, it suggests that human existence must be explored within the sphere of man himself, and thus that the whole concept of descent or determination by natural causes is, at best, of secondary importance. Kant tries to show for instance that the immanent structure of human existence has an impact even on natural factors which would superficially suggest an affinity between man and the animal world. This is the case with sexual attraction. In the animal world, sexual attraction is merely a matter

[25] Gerhard Krüger deals with the anthropological reflections analytically in the context of his exploration of Kant's moral theory. See Gerhard Krüger, *Philosophie und Moral in der Kantischen Kritik*, Tuebingen, J.C.B. Mohr (Paul Siebeck), 1931, p. 37ff. See also Frederick P. Van de Pitte, *Kant as Philosophical Anthropologist*. The Hague, Martinus Nijhoff, 1971, p. 7ff.

[26] In *On History*, p. 54.

of transient, periodic impacts, but man can prolong and even increase attraction by means of the imagination.[27] This is only one example of the way in which natural factors are shaped by the intervention of human qualities – here imagination as a faculty of intelligence if not of reason. The characteristic trait of human history, according to Kant, is that it moves from bondage to instinct to rational control, or, alternatively, from the tutelage of nature to a state of freedom. In other words, it progresses towards perfection. Kant's only concession to natural forces in human history is that history begins from the bottom and not from the top: "The history of nature ... begins with good, for it is the work of God, while the history of freedom begins with wickedness, for it is the work of man ... the individual must consider not only every act of wickedness he commits his own fault, but also all the evils he suffers; yet, at the same time, insofar as he is a member of the whole (a species), he must admire and praise the wisdom and purposiveness of the whole arrangement."[28] Kant is suggesting here that there is a tension between wickedness and goodness, but not between man's subjection to extra-human forces and his obedience to the moral imperative. This distinction is really one between fulfilling a moral destiny and being subject to laws fit for an uncivilized and animal state.[29] This dichotomy between natural and civilized states does not coincide with the distinction indicated in the structure of history between human acts and forms of government, or individual acts and the constant and essential features of historical peoples. If we assume that culture affects mankind's natural functions progressively, it is still not clear whether these natural features include historical conditions of a quasi-permanent nature, like the traits of people, the *Schlag* referred to above to connote a kind or species. Once again, the distinction between man's labours and what is provided by nature cannot cope with the full spectrum of historical reality, since peoples' characters are, at least to some extent, historical manifestations due to human labour rather than to natural forces. They belong to culture and not to man's instinctive equipment.

The only short comment we find in Kant about the collective existence of human beings is that the mixture of human tribes as a result of conquest is in all probability not beneficial to mankind because it gradually abolishes their character. This is so in spite of all the alleged philanthropism.[30] This suggests that the variety of human groups must be maintained during the progress of mankind. However, Kant does not examine the interaction

[27] *Ibid.*, p. 29.
[28] *Ibid.*, p. 60.
[29] *Ibid.*, p. 61 note.
[30] *Anthropologie*, p. 250.

between the diversity of human beings and universal civil society. Kant's theory led him to emphasize man making himself and history. But analytically and descriptively, he was obliged to include factors of human existence which cannot be subsumed under the general heading of "self-activity" and thus are not of character formation within history.

The avenue leading from the moral idea at the top and the avenue leading from the empirical forces at the bottom do not meet. The fact that they do not meet in actuality is explained by the distinction between the empirical and intelligible spheres. They do not meet in Kant's systematic presentation because the distinction between practice as motivated by reason and practice as realized in concrete circumstances must be maintained. This distinction is an unbridgeable chasm, with all that implies for Kant's theory of morals and his theory of practice. The last part of our exploration will re-iterate the basic dilemma of Kant's theory of human action.

CHAPTER SIX

INCENTIVE AND PROPENSITY

1

The problem before us is the impact of the moral law on actual human conduct. In terms of the incentives (*Triebfedern*) of pure practical reason, Kant attributed to the moral law the capacity to determine the will directly.[1] The moral law is an incentive, even though it is impossible for the human reason to discover how a law can be the direct determining ground of the will.[2] The moral law arouses respect: the idea of something as the determining ground of the will demands respect and the moral law is subjectively a cause of respect.[3] The feeling engendered by the moral law cannot be considered either enjoyment or pain. It can be described as an interest in obedience to the law, or as a moral interest. The capacity for taking an interest in the law or respect for the moral law is really the moral feeling (*das moralische Gefühl*).[4] The notion of the incentives was an attempt to achieve two objectives simultaneously: Kant wanted to show that the formulated moral law, grounded as it is in reason, is not separate from human response. This is why he tries to show the transformation of the law into an incentive which gives rise to the human response of respect or interest. While the moral law is formulated on the level of reason, the response is bound to occur on the level of the human partner. The second objective is to show that reason transforms itself into response or feeling without becoming sensuous or pathological, in Kant's terminology, as a result of the transformation. Rationality transforms itself into a response, or its content engenders the attitude towards it. It thus acquires the status of trans-rationality, which means

---

[1] *Kr.d.r.V.*, p. 84; p. 74.
[2] *Ibid.*, p. 85; p. 75.
[3] *Ibid.*, p. 87; p. 77.
[4] *Ibid.*, p. 94; p. 83.

emotion, since Kant apparently assumed that a response could not just be "*ein Fürwahrhalten*," but had to be an attitude.

Incentives, interests and maxims apply only to finite human beings. Hence the question of the immediate impact of respect on human beings who, being finite, are also moved by sensuous propensities. Kant tries to show that there is an a-symmetry between the inclinations of self-love and respect for the moral law as the ground of the determination of the will. If we acknowledge the moral law with all its ramifications for human response, we must take cognizance of the humiliation to our self-consciousness (*demütigt das moralische Gesetz unvermeidlich jeden Menschen*).[5] To put it differently, the moral law checks the propensity to self-esteem, as long as the latter is based on sensibility and not on the moral law. It is in this sense that the moral law strikes down conceit – self-regard, self-love, benevolence toward oneself, or self-satisfaction.[6]

Because of the direct impact of the moral law on self-awareness which is related both to self-esteem and to respect, Kant adduces many examples to show that there is an immediate response to righteousness. My mind, says Kant, bows whether I choose or not, however high I carry my head, that he may not forget my superior position.[7] This is because all good is defective in man. The law made evident in an example always humbles my pride. The man I see before me provides me with a standard. Respect is a tribute I cannot refuse to pay merit (*Verdienst*), whether I will it or not. I pay this tribute even when I outwardly appear to withhold it, for I cannot help feeling it inwardly.[8] This is a telling statement about the impact of the moral law. The directness of the moral law is such that it overpowers us, whether we will or not. A more mitigated version states that the inward response cannot be withheld, even when an attempt is made to withhold its outward expression. The immediate impact of the moral law is sometimes expressed by Kant in the rather far-reaching statement that what we ought to call good must be an object of the faculty of desire in the judgement of every reasonable man. Evil, on the other hand, must be an object of aversion in the eyes of everyone.[9] This is why Kant refers, among other things, to the Stoic who, in his pain, cried out: "Pain, however thou tormentest me, I will never admit that thou art anything bad" (*kakón, malum*). "A single lie of which he was conscious would have struck down his pride (*seinen Mut*), but pain served

---

[5] *Ibid.*, p. 87; p. 77.
[6] *Ibid.*, p. 85–86; p. 75–76.
[7] *Ibid.*, p. 90; p. 79.
[8] *Ibid.*, p. 90; p. 80.
[9] *Ibid.*, p. 72; p. 62–63.

only as an occasion for raising it ..."[10] The immediate impact of the moral law leads to an immediate awareness of the distinction between pain and evil. The awareness clearly relates to respect for the moral law, but its repercussions do not merely humble conceit; humbling the person to the point where he distinguishes between his own immediate physical pain and evil which has a trans-egotistic content. This is but one of the examples where Kant tried to show that the response generated by the moral imperative oversteps the inward attitude and leads to a particular form of behaviour. After all, the Stoic behaves in a certain way: he does not yield to the pain, but expresses his refusal to succumb to the situation which only partially overpowers him.

Yet such examples remain within the sphere of personal self-awareness; there are no examples from the public or historical spheres. This matter will now be more closely examined by exploring Kant's description of *Achtung* or respect in his *Metaphysik der Sitten*.

2

Respect is constantly related to the frailty (*fragilitas*) of human nature.[11] Kant probably thought the whole concept of duty and its concomitants is central, because without duty and its response there would be no way of overcoming this basic human frailty. Respect is a response to the humanity (*die Menschheit*) in other people which can be demanded from every one.[12] It is precisely because respect and duty on the one hand and the frailty on the other are central, that their limitations become prominent as well. The first point to be made here concerns the relation and distinction between love and respect. Both are feelings which accompany the realization or the performance of duties. But they can exist and be seen separately as well, as in the following statement: Love they neighbour in spite of the fact that he deserves little respect. A man must be respected even if he does not deserve to be loved.[13]

The duty to love one's neighbour is the duty to make another man's ends my ends, as long as his ends do not defy morality. The duty to respect one's neighbour is entailed in the maxim not to demote any man to a means to my own ends. In other words, the other man should not give himself up to

---

[10] *Ibid.*, p. 71; p. 62.
[11] *Met.d.S.*, p. 259.
[12] *Ibid.*, p. 279.
[13] *Ibid.*, p. 297.

serve my ends.[14] This significant statement clearly indicates the fact that love is a positive imperative which is more forthcoming than the imperative of respect. Love is intended to make one's fellow man's ends one's own, whereas respect has the negative connotation implied in the maxim which forbids turning one's fellow man into a means for one's ends. Respect is anti-egoistic, while love is by definition altruistic. Kant says that the negative aspect of respect is essentially a prohibition from being supercilious towards others, or the duty not to encroach on the domain of others (*niemandem das Seine zu schmälern*). Similarly, omission of the duty of love is a non-virtue (*Untugend – peccatum*, probably with the religious associations of the term "*peccatum*") whereas omission of the duty of respect is a vice (*vitium*).[15] The vices related to undermining the respect due to others are pride, libel and ridicule (*die Verhöhnung*).[16] The distinction between love and respect is expressed differently when Kant says that love refers to the other man's ends, whereas respect refers to his rights.[17] Rights are related to man *qua* man, whereas the end is related to one's willingness to understand another human being specifically. It is therefore not accidental that Kant goes so far as to say that the duty to respect man is grounded in the logical use of reason. Contempt (*contemnere*) contradicts this duty, because it contradicts the respect which is due to men in general.[18] Another way of formulating the difference is that respect relates to the very definition and place of the human beings in the inter-human context, whereas love is grounded in particular relationships between particular human beings. Hence Kant says that the principle of mutual love cannot but make human beings closer, whereas the respect they owe each other keeps the distance between them.[19]

These descriptions and juxtapositions clearly indicate the fact that Kant was aware that respect is not the only possible response to the imperative.

[14] *Ibid.*, p. 299.
[15] *Ibid.*, p. 317.
[16] *Ibid.*, p. 317–320.
[17] *Ibid.*, p. 347.
[18] *Ibid.*, p. 315.
[19] *Ibid.*, p. 298.
   With regard to contempt, Kant still distinguishes between moral contempt and the attitude entertained by people in the sphere he calls "*bürgerlich*," which seems to represent not so much the civil aspect of life as the pecuniary and commercial aspect. It is because of this distinction that Kant quotes Pope's epistle III entitled "Of the Use of Riches" (*Moral Essays*, III, 371–374) in German translation: On the demon who sinks deep within the person and possesses him, eventually secures his soul. Kant translates this phrase as "*sich seiner Seele bemächtigt.*" What is significant from the point of view of our analysis is the distinction between the moral and the commercial attitude, since according to Kant, commercial achievements, as Pope characterizes them, do not engender contempt but admiration of the person who shows commercial wisdom (*Handelsweisheit*).

Moreover, respect has predominantly negative connotations, since it calls for the feeling of superiority to other people to be overcome. Kant probably also thought that respect is a direct response, grounded in the recognition of man as man without regard to the particular situation and the specific ends of the person involved. One of the manifestations of the immediate character of the response of respect is self-contempt when a person does not obey the imperative to respect. Hence self-evaluation is inherent in one's response to the response, or more specifically, in the omission to respond to respect which in turn is the response to the moral imperative. From this point of view, the strength and weakness of the duty of respect are two sides of the same coin.

It must be reiterated that neither respect nor love create a public domain, a realm of actual human beings, and not only a realm of ends in Kant's sense of the word. Respect is an attitude towards every human being as a representative of mankind at large. Love is grounded in the recognition of specific human beings and of their specific ends. The question arises as to whether actual deeds follow from either of these attitudes, and there is a very telling statement about this: The respect to which I am bound by nature is respect for the law – what Kant calls "*reverere legem*." This also means obeying the law in relation to other men. But respect does not mean revering other men or what Kant calls "*reverentia adversus hominem*." Neither is it a universal and unconditional duty for men to do something vis-à-vis other human beings.[20] Kant thought apparently that the theory of virtues which is grounded in principles of pure reason can create the underlying attitude of respect or of love. But the transition from the attitude to deeds – "*etwas zu leisten*" – goes beyond the attitude grounded in the moral imperative. If this is true of the basic attitude and of the interrelation between human beings grounded in the recognition of mankind, the *a fortiori* conclusion will be that historical acts and the historical sphere in general do not originate in this basic attitude to mankind. Indeed Kant did not escape this conclusion.

3

The motivation Kant calls *Sittsamkeit* connotes decency and morality. Kant describes it as the inclination to inspire others with respect for us (*Achtung gegen uns einflössen*). *Sittsamkeit* also means good manners, which Kant

[20] *Ibid.*, p. 321.

describes as concealment of that which might inspire lack of esteem. The behaviour described by the generic term *Sittsamkeit* is the real basis of all true sociability – *Geselligkeit*.[21] This statement indicates respect or *Achtung* not for the moral law and for the humanity implied in every human being, but respect in the inter-personal context. The question is to what extent Kant is referring to respect, or to holding someone in respect and esteeming him. These may eventually lead, to say the least, to the threshold of vanity on part of the esteemed person.

This is not mere conjecture, since in the Fourth Thesis of the *Idea for a Universal History*, Kant specifically refers to man's inclination to associate with others in terms of what he calls man's unsocial sociability. This paradoxical description indicates man's propensity to enter into society and the mutual opposition among men, which constantly threatens to break up society. One of the manifestations of man's unsocial character is his wish to have everything his own way. Man finds himself opposed on all sides, because he knows that he, too, is inclined to oppose others. This dual state of antagonistic association in the framework of association awakens all men's powers and makes him conquer his inclination to be lazy. He is propelled by vainglory, lust for power and avarice, to achieve a status among his fellows. He has an ambivalent attitude towards them too: he can neither tolerate them nor withdraw from them. Without these unsociable characteristics which are unalienable because they are related to man's selfishness, all talents would remain hidden, or, as Kant puts it, unborn in an Arcadian pastoral or idyllic shepherd's life, characterized by comfort, contentment, and mutual affection. As good-natured as the sheep they herd, men would hardly have more worth than their beasts. Hence the competitive vanity, the insatiable desire to possess and to rule, which amount to incompatibilities among men, lead to an end which mankind is supposed to achieve. Here nature is wiser than man's primary inclination, since man desires comfort while nature desires discord, which is manifest in the selfish propensities exhibited in the inter-personal realm.[22]

It is necessary to distinguish in the text paraphrased above between motivations, however evil, which serve good objectives in spite of themselves and the character of the intentions. Vanity and the urge for power are viewed by Kant as dynamic forces of human behaviour, whereas sociable inclinations are placed under the heading of laziness or dormancy. The dynamic character of human behaviour and the forces of the historical-public sphere differ from the respect engendered by the moral law in the private domain.

[21] Conjectural Beginning of Human History, *On History*, p. 57.
[22] Idea of Universal History, *On History*, p. 15–16.

The esteem implied in vanity, which is after all an urge to gain esteem under false pretenses, is by no means fortuitous. Vanity presupposes the interpersonal context; it is a selfish urge inasmuch as it refers to the ego driven by the urge, but it is meaningless unless there are other egos who respond by granting the desired esteem. Kant is aware of the evil character of the urges whose dynamic quality he acknowledges and approves. This comes to the fore in his discussion in *Anthropologie* under the heading of "Inclinations to Gain Influence over other People." Under this general heading Kant deals specifically with honour, power, and money, and concomitantly with vanity, the lust for dominance and avarice (*Ehrsucht, Herrschsucht und Habsucht*). Vanity is the human weakness which makes it possible to influence men through their opinions; the lust for dominance exerts influence through fear, while avarice appeals to men's interest, which in this context means material interest. Vanity is not just a love of honour, but a striving for repute (*Ehrenruf*) which stops short at the mere appearance of repute (*wo es am Schein genug ist*). As to the lust for dominance, Kant says that this is an unjust passion. It originates in the fear of being dominated by others and aspires to have the advantage of them in time to dominate them. This is an objectionable and unjust means of making other men serve one's intentions. It is also imprudent because it provokes opposition. The invention of money, which created avarice, is ultimately mere possession without pleasure, on the assumption that possession entails power.[23] This indicates that Kant was aware of the negative moral character of dynamic forces. But he continues to hold the view that the dynamic character of these forces makes them unavoidable in historical existence.

There is a difference between Kant's evaluation of pride and vanity as human characteristics, and his description and evaluation of them as historical forces. Kant's position differs from that taken in the extensive literature on pride and vanity; let us quote just a few statements by Pascal: "We would never take a sea-voyage that we could not afterwards talk about, for the mere pleasure of seeing sights with no hope of ever describing them to others." "*Vanity*. It is very strange that anything so evident as the vanity of the world should be so unknown that if one points out the foolishness of pursuing greatness, one is considered surprising and odd." "Few speak humbly of humility or chastity; few speak doubtingly of scepticism. We are nothing but falsehood, duplicity and contradiction; we conceal and disguise ourselves from ourselves."[24] It was not enough for Kant to indicate the negative character

---

[23] *Anthropologie*, p. 189ff.
[24] Consult: Blaise Pascal, *The Pensées*, translated with an introduction by J.M. Cohen, Penguin Books, 1961, p. 72, 78, 80.

of the features at issue, because men are involved in a basic contradiction between the possibility of coming to a moral standstill and the need to ensure an ongoing historical process.

A parallel to this is to be found in the self-defeating human characteristics which make the attainment of happiness impossible. There is a clash between happiness and culture. Man's nature is not so constituted as to rest satisfied in any possession or enjoyment. Even external nature is far from having made man a particular favourite. In so far as destructive forces are concerned like plague, famine, etc., nature has as little spared man as any other animal. But in addition to the natural forces outside man, there are natural tendencies within him, which lead him to misfortunes of his own invention. Even though we might suppose that nature would have directed human beings to the happiness of their species, this happiness can never be attained in a system of terrestrial nature, because human nature is not capable of it. What therefore remains to man is a formal or subjective condition, the aptitude to set himself ends. The main aptitude is the production in a rational being of any ends whatever of his own choosing, and that aptitude is culture. Only culture can be the ultimate end attributable to nature in respect to the human race.[25]

There is a discrepancy between happiness as a situation of achievement and tranquility and culture as a process related to ends which are not given but deliberately posited. Parallel to this discrepancy is the discrepancy between the incentive grounded in the moral law, which at best leads to a personal self-evaluation and at worst to contempt for human beings who do not follow the moral imperative, and historical or empirical forces. From this point of view it can be said that Kant does not assume a harmony in disharmony, or a disharmony in harmony, insofar as the public sphere of human existence is concerned. He does not assume a harmony between human affections either. This again has to be placed in its proper context, and this will be the next subject for analysis.

4

Kant's basic position could not lead him to the view that man is essentially a social being – and we shall see the bearing of this view when we come to sum

---

On the problem of self-esteem, pride and vanity consult: Arthur O. Lovejoy, *Reflections on Human Nature*, The Johns Hopkins Press, Baltimore, 1961. Lovejoy refers to Kant only briefly on p. 192–193.

[25] We refer here to our preceding analysis of happiness, chapter II.

up the various aspects of Kant's evaluation of social and historical existence. Neither could Kant take the view that passions suffice to explain man's unsocial features, whereas positive affections would come to the fore in human sociability. This is because Kant cannot rely on affections to nourish sociability, for sociability is grounded in man's recognition of his fellow men and of mankind at large and thus in the moral incentive and not in psychological propensities.

Kant's position must be seen against the broader background not so much of a detailed history of ideas as of approaches to the interplay between man's inclinations and his attachment to society. Let us start with a comment from Shaftesbury. Shaftesbury assumes a passion for self-good along with a natural affection for mankind. There is thus an equilibrium of affections and whatever is done from what Shaftesbury calls "any unequal affection" is iniquitous, wicked and wrong. Moreover, there is the admiration and love of order, harmony and proportion. Admiration improves the temper, benefits social affection and greatly assists virtue – which in turn is nothing but the love of order and beauty in society. Any appearance of order attracts the mind and draws the affections. This is true even of the meanest subjects of the world and even more so if the order of the world itself appears just and beautiful. Translated into the human context – there is a constant relation to the interest of a species or to common nature, and there is ultimately an equilibrium of affections between those going towards common nature or what is called the System of the kind and those who regard private nature or the Self-system. In conclusion Shaftesbury states that the wisdom of the ruler who is first and chief in nature has made it to accord with the private interest and good of everyone to work towards the general good.[26]

Shaftesbury's view represents a harmonistic approach to human affections, although this statement calls for a qualification: Shaftesbury assumes an equal distribution of the affections directed to oneself and to mankind. Yet he assumes that concern for the good of mankind, grounded as it is in admiration for the order of the universe, is nevertheless an egoistic or utilitarian component, in that it benefits the agent to care for mankind. The two positions coexist, and it is hard to find any attempt to go beyond their mere coexistence. In any case, man's sociability is grounded in his affections, not only in his needs.

It is reasonable to assume that Kant knew at least some of Ferguson's

---

[26] Shaftesbury, *Characteristicks*, vol. II, An Inquiry concerning Virtue and Merit: The Moralists; a Philosophical Rhapsody, Printed in the Year MDCCXXXII. Consult pages: 25, 31.

writings. The emphasis on sociability is central in Ferguson too. Ferguson says this about man: though a predatory animal, devoted by need or inclination to hunting or war, he is nevertheless highly sociable and fitted to civil life.[27] This statement does not make affections the source of human behaviour, but the generally sociable character of human existence and even its civil character (in the sense of *bürgerliche Gesellschaft* or civil society), which are also central in Kant's socio-political writings, are evidently present here.

Kant could not follow this line, as has already been said, because he thought empirical human existence motivated by ambivalent forces, of which man's propensity for sociability is only one. Moreover, grounding attachment to humanity in inclinations would be, for Kant, a descriptive characterization of human behaviour which does not *ipso facto* contain moral significance. The question Kant faced could therefore be formulated as: whether it is possible to ground sociability in the response to moral law, which means to base it on the recognition of every human being as a person belonging to mankind and thus to the realm of ends. There is a tendency in Kant to translate sociability into an awareness grounded in mutual recognition. This tendency raises the question discussed earlier about motivations leading to deeds which cannot be subsumed under the heading of mutual recognition.

A comparison of Kant's view of empirical human existence with Bayle's is apposite here. Bayle argues against the representatives of one-sided political ideas by comparing them with mathematicians. The latter attempt to apply the results of their investigations of points and lines to concrete material. They are not aware of the fact that geometric entities are only ideas of our spirit. The products of our spirit do not resemble concrete human existence whose essential powers are passions of a different sort. Hence one has to consider the *raison de passion*, not only the *passion de raison*. Kant

---

[27] Adam Ferguson, *Grundsätze der Moralphilosophie*, übersetzt und mit einigen Anmerkungen versehen von Christian Garve, Frankfurt und Leipzig, p. 12. Garve, whose relations with Kant are rather complex, refers in his Notes to his translation to what he calls *vernünftige Begierden*, which are juxtaposed to animal urges (*tierische Begierden*). The distinction which he suggests is the following: all urges indicating things which merely evoke feelings (*Empfindungen*) are animal urges. Other urges which give rise to actions are called reasonable urges. The urge for power, money, vanity would be listed among the former. See also Ferguson's text in the German translation, where the reference is to *die vernünftigen Triebe*. Listed among these are concern for self-subsistence, love between parents and children, attraction between the sexes, but also the inclination to sociability and the urge to obtain preference (*die Begierde nach Vorzug*, p. 42). The text quoted from a 1787 edition appears to be a second edition of the book, though this is not mentioned on the front page.

does not argue like Bayle that there is an abstract theory which falls short of concrete behaviour. On the contrary, he describes human behaviour in its concreteness. A theory of human behaviour is not ideal human behaviour but practical philosophy and all that which goes with this discipline.[28]

On these issues Kant comes close to some of the views expressed by Montesquieu. Among the vices mentioned by Montesquieu, we find ambition and idleness; meanness mixed with pride; the desire for riches without industry, etc. Montesquieu specifically mentions vanity as advantageous to a government, and pride as dangerous to it. Innumerable benefits result from vanity, like industry, the arts, fashions, politeness, and taste. Yet there are also infinite evils which spring from the pride of certain nations, like laziness, poverty, and a total neglect of everything. Laziness is the effect of pride, while labour is a consequence of vanity. And indeed, Montesquieu mentions Spaniards whose pride leads them to decline labour, while the vanity of the Frenchmen leads them to work better than others. But the systematic consequence Montesquieu draws from these reflections is a distinction between the political sphere and the moral sphere. Montesquieu is careful to insist that this is not meant to lessen the infinite distance which must ever exist between virtue and vice. He wants his readers to understand that all political vices are not moral vices, and that all moral vices are not political vices. Those who make laws which shock the general spirit of a nation ought not to be ignorant of this. The distinction Montesquieu suggests between the moral and the political spheres can perhaps be substituted by the Kantian distinction between the moral sphere and historical existence – together with the forces operating in it. In Kant the political sphere is probably to some extent – and we have seen this in terms of regimes, wars and even education – an intermediate sphere which, because it is structured, is more conducive to the response to moral imperatives than natural existence. Here we come back to a comparison between Aristotle and Kant, this time to the nature of friendship in both systems. This will be considered from the broader perspective of the interpretation of human nature in both thinkers. This will be the last part of our analysis of Kant's philosophy of practice.[29]

---

[28] See the article on Hobbes in the Dictionary.

Rudolf Eucken's essay: Bayle und Kant, eine Studie (in *Beiträge zur Einführung in die Geschichte der Philosophie*, Leipzig, Verlag der Dürr'schen Buchhandlung, 1906, p. 82ff.) contains several of the pertinent quotations from Bayle, though the context of the analysis does not touch on the basic issues involved.

[29] Baron de Montesquieu, *The Spirit of the Laws*, translated by Thoman Nugent, with an introduction by Franz Neumann, New York, Haffner Publishing Company, 1949, vol. I, p. 24, 295–296, 297.

5

Let us summarize briefly some of the points Aristotle makes in relation to friendship, because in the questions of detail there is an affinity between Kant and Aristotle. Aristotle distinguishes between different kinds of friendship, emphasizing the importance of mutual feelings between people, since goodwill is not enough. He shows that there are corresponding forms of love and friendship. There is mutual respect and mutually recognized love. Those who love each other wish each other well. In this sense love is a form of friendship. Those who love each other for their utility do not love each other for themselves, but in virtue of some good which they obtain from each other. Here a distinction must be made between those who love for the sake of utility and therefore love for what is good for themselves, and those who love for the sake of pleasure. These modes of love are only incidental since the man loved is not loved as a person but for the good or pleasure he provides. There is a kind of friendship mainly between old people and those who are in their prime or young, or those who are hosts and guests respectively. Aristotle says that the young are pleasant to each other only in so far as they arouse in each other the hope of something good to come. Young people are guided by emotion and therefore quickly become friends and quickly cease to be so. For Aristotle, perfect friendship is the friendship of men who are good and are alike in virtue. Such friends are alike in wishing each other well. They are good without qualification and by being so, they are useful to each other. They are pleasant too since the good which they represent is pleasant without qualification. Their activities are pleasurable. Such friendship is permanent although it is only natural for it to be rare because people who have the character for this mode of friendship are rare.

We have seen that Aristotle indicates a kinship between love and friendship and that his criterium for the scale of friendship is the connecting link between the friends and the concomitant permanence of friendship. The more friendship is based on goodness which in turn engenders pleasure and utility, the higher the friendship and the more permanent it is. Thus for Aristotle equality and likeness are implied in friendship, since the similarity of those who are alike in virtue is the most stable connecting factor among human beings. Aristotle also indicates the kinship between friendship and justice: when men are friends they have no need of justice. This should probably be understood in the sense that they do not need an external principle to govern their relations. But when they are just, they need friendship, and the truest form of justice is thought to be a friendly quality. Friendship therefore contains the quality of justice but adds to it the particular, let us call it, human touch which colours the objective framework of justice. Yet it can be said that the existence of justice in a community is a precondition or substratum for friendship, for there is thought to be some form of justice as well as of friendship in every community. Particular kinds of friendships – and here Aristotle does not elaborate the point by referring to the modes of friendship alluded to before – correspond to particular kinds of community. All forms of community are like parts of the political community; hence the political community is the precondition for friendship. Friendship is a specific elaboration and continuation of the human existence which is the life of the community. There is a line of continuity between man's political nature and his natural desire to live with his fellows and man's involvement in a friendship, in spite of the fact that there is a hierarchy of different sorts of friendship. The emphasis on man's sociability is not made obsolete by what Aristotle says: "Indeed, it is generally true that it is a difficult business for men to live together and to be partners in any form of human activity, but it is especially difficult to do so when property is involved."[30] This statement should probably be seen as an empirical assessment of human conduct in spite of men's basic sociability. To be sure, friendship of any kind runs counter to the difficulties of human cooperation indicated here. Even though it emerges from men's political character, it is by no means an omnipresent form of human existence.

In conclusion, then, Aristotle considers friendship a virtue or implying a virtue. But it is most necessary to living besides. Aristotle combines goodness and utility in spite of his tendency to evaluate goodness *per se* as a factor in friendship as better than a friendship based on utility. In any case, men are more able to think and to act with friends – and these two activities have an intrinsic quality as well as an instrumental one. Because Aristotle is never oblivious to the instrumental quality of friendship he says that friendship seems to hold states together, and that lawgivers care more for friendship than for justice. Factionalism is the worst enemy of cooperation, and lawgivers therefore consider it their worst enemy. Here too Aristotle is ambivalent, since in a sense justice for the existence of states seems to be a minimal condition while friendship is a maximal condition. Aristotle also wavers between the view that friendship is a form of justice and the view that both are independent factors of human cohesion.

The question of the specific motivation underlying friendship recurs in Aristotle. Thus he says that goodwill is a friendly relation but one which is not identical with friendship. This is because one can have goodwill both

[30] *The Politics of Aristotle,* translated with an introduction, notes, and appendices by Ernest Barker, Oxford, at the Clarendon Press, 1946, 1262b, p. 49.

towards people one knows and towards those one does not know, but there can be no friendship without knowing people. It could be said, and this is probably the most that can be said, in the context that goodwill is inactive friendship, although it becomes friendship when it is prolonged and reaches the point of intimacy. Aristotle even applies the notion and the qualities of friendship to what he calls man's relation to himself. Man is his own best friend and therefore ought to love himself best. This sort of self-love must be viewed more specifically as love for one's own nobility: the good man loves the noble part of himself. The good man assigns to himself the greater share of what is noble, and it has therefore been said that a man should love himself because it makes him love nobility, even though this is only a higher and loftier sort of self-love.

Thus Aristotle struggled with the problem of finding a motivation for friendship: on the one hand he relates friendship to justice, on the other he relates it to love. Friendship is more than mere justice, and indeed it is close to love. Hence the questions dealt with by Aristotle relate to the nature of love. Since Aristotle gives love the highest place on his scale, he is led to assume that man's relation to himself, and to his own goodness which implies affirmation of himself, is a form of love and hence a form of friendship. This reasoning led Aristotle to what seems a paradoxical conclusion or description, namely that man is his own friend. Indeed, and we are repeating what has been said before, all these reflections are formulated on the assumption of man's basic sociability or his political nature.[31]

A preliminary observation is called for when we now turn to Kant. As we have seen, Kant does not begin from the assumption of man's basic sociability, since man's nature contains both sociability and unsociability. Friendship cannot be based on this, man's ambiguous nature. Indeed Kant places friendship in the context of respect, though he speaks of the most intimate unification of love and respect in friendship. Here again it must be said that man's attachment to humanity is not based on his nature but on his obedience to the moral law. In this context, friendship can only be viewed as uniting two persons by equal and mutual love and respect. But since respect is present in Kant's analysis of friendship, Kant speaks of the duty of friendship, a concept which would be inconceivable in the context of affections alone. Respect looms large in friendship. One of the manifestations of the friendship motivated by respect is therefore that even the best of friends should not demean themselves (*sich gemein machen*).

---

[31] The resume of Aristotle's exploration of the nature of friendship is based on *The Nicomachean Ethics*, books eight and nine. The wording follows by and large the above mentioned translation by Ross.

Since Kant considers friendship in the context of the moral law and not in the context of human nature in the Aristotelian sense, he is bound to follow the stringent line of his moral considerations and to exclude any possible utilitarian outcome from friendship. Friendship, he says, unites two persons who seek their mutual advantage. Friendship has to be moral in the pure sense of the term. And mutual support in case of need should neither be the end nor the motivating ground for friendship.

Because the point of departure lies in the notion of the moral law and in the incentive of respect, Kant suggests that the distinction between mutual love and friendship should even be applied to the relation pertaining between a benefactor and a beneficiary. The latter has the duty of gratitude. The relation of mutual love exists between the two, but this love differs from friendship since friendship implies mutual respect, and this respect is lacking in the relationship between benefactor and beneficiary. Kant emphasizes the equality between men implied in friendship, and faces the problem of turning this notion into an intimate motivation which is "taken to heart" (*Beherzigung*). Aristotle, as we have seen, emphasized the similarity between the two friends, but that this similarity had to be understood as a relation between kindred spirits. Kant clearly replaces the similarity by the idea of equality, thus grounding friendship in common humanity in its universal sense, and not in the proximity or kinship existing between two people.

Aristotle showed a continuum from friendship based on utility to friendship based on virtues. As a result of the dichotomy between inclinations and moral law, Kant cannot assume a continuity from what he calls pragmatic friendship (which is friendship based, on ends human beings attempt to attain), and friendship (which is related to philanthropy in the strict sense of the term – *Menschenfreund* – friendship for the whole human species). Precisely because he transposes friendship from the small and intimate circle of individual people to the broad scope of humanity, Kant faced the problem of the principle of selection: how are friends chosen from the broadest range of humanity? Here the emphasis on love does not help, since love too is addressed to mankind at large and not to specific human beings in the here and now. For Aristotle who starts from human inclinations and moves towards mutual human appreciation and mutual affirmation between people, the question of selecting the individuals among whom friendship pertains was not such an acute problem. As we indicated before, Aristotle certainly faced the problem of the relationship between justice and friendship. He probably made the question too complicated for himself by trying to find links between phenomena and principles which possibly are not necessarily connected. The fact that Aristotle tried to establish these relations is to be explained by the basic presupposition that mutual friendship is a mode of human sociability. Be that as it may, Aristotle begins with the basic and moves to the more elaborate specific and intimate phenomenon. On the other hand, Kant in his usual way starts from the top, from mankind, from the recognition of mankind, from respect for humanity; hence for him the question of the selection or individuation of people among whom friendship obtains becomes essential and initial. The moral system provides for the reference to the human species but not for the reference to a specific human being. On the contrary, in so far as the operative translation of the reference to mankind at large manifests itself in the recognition of the principle of equality, the phenomenon of friendship remains inexplicable. From the point of view of equality, all human beings are equal and the closed or selective character of friendship lacks any basis whatsoever. Hence it is imperative to consider the question of whether Kant suggests any principles of exclusion to explain the existence of intimate relations between human beings, and this after all is the essential feature of friendship. We shall now look into that question.

6

Let us begin this part of our exposition by an attempt to show the reasons which led Kant to exclude affection, let alone passions, from the relationship and attitude of friendship. A clue is to be found in one of Kant's many descriptions of the affections which, he says, are merely related to feeling; passions belong to the faculty of desire. They are therefore inclinations which make all determinability of the elective will by principles impossible. This is clearly Kant's most important argument, namely that there is a basic contradiction between the will which is determined or determinable by principles and inclinations which handicap that determinability. After all, will relates to choice while inclinations create a situation in which the agent is swept away by overpowering factors. And indeed Kant goes on to view affections and passions as a gradual escalation of subjection to overpowering factors. Affections are impetuous and irresponsible, while passions are abiding and deliberate. For example, anger which represents resentment is to be listed as an affection, whereas resentment which takes the form of hatred or vindictiveness is a passion. The freedom of the mind is impeded in affection, whereas it is abrogated in passion.[32]

---

[32] *Kr.d.U.*, p. 119 note; p. 124 note.

Affection is the surprise created by sensation which deprives the mind of its equilibrium (*die Fassung des Gemüts – animus sui compos*). Affection exhibits itself quickly, as in wrath for instance: it does not occur speedily, it does not occur at all, and it also forgets easily. The passion of hatred takes time to strike deep roots. Passion is like water bursting through a dam, or like a river wearing its way and more deeply into its bed. Affection is like intoxication (*Rausch*); it subsides after sleep, whereas passion is a mania (*Wahnsinn*) brooding over a representation which engraves itself more and more deeply.[33]

Love is discussed in the context of affection and passion. A man who loves retains his faculty of sight, but one who falls in love (*sich verliebt*) inevitably becomes blind to the shortcomings of the loved one.[34] Because love is placed among the affections or passions, it cannot occupy a central position in the ethical domain. Here Kant is sharpening the dichotomy between the discipline of reason and the motivation by love. He emphasizes that the command to love God means that respect is required for a law which commands love instead of leaving it to arbitrary choice, and this means that love is made a principle. This is particularly clear in the reference to love of God, since as an inclination this love is impossible for God is not an object of the senses. This kind of love is possible among human beings, but here it cannot be commanded, for it is not possible for men to love someone on command. In this sense to love God means to like to do his commandments; to love one's neighbour means to like to do all one's duties towards him. In the ethical context the ideal would be totally separate from desires and inclinations; the latter rest on physical causes and do not agree with the moral law which has an entirely different source.[35]

To be sure, and this has to be re-emphasized, Kant's attitude to the passions is not unequivocal. We have seen that Kant grants the importance of motivations grounded in passions for the historical process. Elsewhere he mentions Pope's verse, which he renders in German: "Ist die Vernunft nun ein Magnet, so sind die Leidenschaften Winde." This is probably the – non-literal – German equivalent of the verse in "Essay on Man" II, 108: "Reason is the card but passion is the gale." Kant's reservation or criticism of this saying is unconvincing; he says that one can forgive a poet this saying, whereas a philosopher cannot admit this principle even in order to praise the passions as a temporary provision, which providence has intentionally

---

[33] *Anthropologie*, p. 165–166.
[34] *Ibid.*
[35] *Kr.d.p.V.*, p. 96ff; 85ff.

lodged in the human species before it has reached an adequate level of culture.[36]

The fact that Kant came to include love in the ethical sphere does not change its fundamental systematic position, since he refers to the duty of loving one's neighbour. This duty relates to the well-being (*Wohlsein – salus*) of human beings; a person who observes this duty finds satisfaction in well-being and loves men; he is, in short, a philanthropist. But specific manifestations of the duties of love lack the component of affection. These manifestations are beneficence (*Wohltätigkeit*), to help others who are in need to happiness without hoping for a reward; the duty of gratitude, which for Kant is veneration of a person for a good he has done us. The important point to stress here is that the feeling which Kant indicates is connected with this evaluation, is respect for one's fellow man. He refers to veneration and not, let us say, to attachment. This is why in his description of gratitude Kant emphasizes that respect is felt by the person to whom a good deed has been done, while the person doing the good deed has an attitude of love. The third manifestation of love is what Kant calls participation (*Teilnehmung*) which he describes as "*Mit-freude*" and "*Mitleid*" (*sympathia moralis*; shared joy and shared sorrow). Kant is not unaware of pleasure and pain as the sensuous feeling present in a sympathetic attitude. Yet he attempts to transpose the feeling of shared joy and shared sorrow to the level of the humane – *Menschlichkeit – humanitas*; he even tries to adopt the Stoic ideal of the wise man: I desire a friend not so that he would assist me in poverty, illness, or imprisonment, but so that I can stand by him and save a person. This Stoic version is obviously Kant's attempt to eradicate the affections, as much as possible, from shared sorrow or pity and to stress the outgoingness, which recognizes a person's need without any reciprocity being expected.[37]

All this has been said to explain the fact that Kant does not include affections, let alone passions, in friendship. This is why he does not include any sort of pleasure, however elevated, in friendship either and why he does not follow the line suggested by Aristotle. What then is left of friendship? Kant describes moral friendship as the mutual trust between two persons. Two people are open to one another and they disclose their hidden judgments and feelings, in so far as this openness is compatible with mutual respect. Here the emphasis is already on confidence rather than affection, and on the inner connection of friendship and veracity: in friendship a person can disclose his judgments and feelings without losing the respect of the other because of the nature and content of the two. Kant is presupposing

---

[36] *Anthropologie*, p. 184–185.
[37] *Met.d.S.*, p. 302ff.

man's double nature here. Men are social and unsocial at the same time, as we have seen time and again. Man's sociability opens him to his fellow-man. But he is also afraid that the other will abuse the disclosure of his thoughts, and this is why he is forced to conceal a good many of his judgments, mainly those relating to other men. Man's fear of disclosing his views is therefore grounded in his awareness of man's unsocial nature which manifest itself in a possible abuse of revealed secrets. Yet at the same time man's social nature makes him wish to exchange his views with somebody, views related – interestingly enough – not only to other people, but also to the government, religion and so forth. He is in a quandary between these two attitudes because he is afraid that his confidence will be abused to his detriment. He would also like to be open about his own shortcomings and failures, but here too he is afraid that their disclosure will impair the respect in which others may hold him.[38]

This is where the phenomenon of friendship finds its justification and its *differentia specifica*: a man can air his thoughts once he finds a person endowed both with a good moral attitude and with reason. He can open his heart to such a person with full trust, without apprehending any danger. Man is not alone and imprisoned with his thoughts. In his openness he enjoys the freedom which he lacks as long as he is locked up in himself. This sort of friendship is rare but it is not merely an ideal since the black swan actually exists here and there in all its perfection.[39]

In so far as Kant sought the principle of selection or exclusion characteristic of the establishment of a friendship, he found it in trustworthiness and not in affection. Trustworthiness in turn is not related to the expectations a person may form of the deeds or performances to be expected from a trusted person. The person trusted is a partner in human communication or in a human dialogue, based on veracity and on openness. Hence friendship as an insulated human contact is ultimately related to truth, with all the value related to it in Kant's ethics. Man has a right to his own veracity, i.e. to the subjective truth expressing his own person. Veracity in one's utterances is everyone's formal duty towards others, whatever the personal disadvantages.[40] Yet there is a clash between the inescapable validity of the maxim of truth and the human situation in which the disadvantage to the agent is taken into consideration. Friendship for Kant is therefore not an

---

[38] Hence friendship is basically related to uprightness and sincerity. On sincerity in Kant consult for instance: *Religion*, p. 178, note.

[39] *Met.d.S.*, p. 326ff.

[40] Über Ein Vermeintes Recht Aus Menschenliebe Zu Lügen, *Sämtliche Werke*, vol. VI, ed. by Karl Vorländer, Leipzig, 1913, p. 202.

expression of an attitude or affection, but a device to safeguarding behaviour according to the maxim of truth through man's sociability. In a sense Kant sees friendship as a situation in which truth and trustfulness are realized *in acto*. At the same time friendship is the empirical guarantee for behaviour according to the command of truth. On the one hand there is a concession to the limitations imposed on behaviour according to the maxim of truth by the invidious aspect of human nature. But on the other Kant envisages a situation where the sociable manifestations of human nature converge with the maxim of truth or at least meet it in the actual human condition.

This is probably the most Kant could assume as far as the shift from the moral law to concrete human deeds is concerned. To assume more would involve Kant in empirical modes of behaviour, and they had to be left aside. The absence of those empirical considerations explains the difficulties built into the realization of practice. To this Kant's own words are a suitable finale:

The rule for the practical use of reason according to this Idea, therefore, intends to express nothing more than that we must take our maxims as if, in all its changes from good to better which proceed into the infinite, our moral state, with respect to its disposition (the *homo noumenon*, "whose changes take place in heaven") would not be subjected at all to temporal change.[41]

---

[41] The End of All Things, in *On History*, p. 78.

CHAPTER SEVEN

EXCURSUS:
BETWEEN EPICURUS AND STOA

1

Kant approaches the traditional juxtaposition between Epicurus and the
Stoa in two contexts – the first can be described as typological, the second
as analytical and critical. The distinction between the two approaches is
clear, but nevertheless the typological presentation has some bearing on the
analytical and critical one. We will therefore start with the typology and
move on to the critical analysis.

Kant first contrasts Epicurus and Plato by classifying the Epicurean
system as empiricism and the Platonic as indicating what he describes as
"intuitive knowledge." With all provisions and hesitations, he sums up the
Epicurean position as follows: the cognitive task is to explain appearances.
We must assume the material composing the world to be such that we learn
about it from experience and from experience only. Because of this centrality
of experience and because our task is confined to explaining appearances,
we must proceed from the assumption that the field of our enquiry will not
be circumscribed by any limit or by the beginning of the world. It should
already be noted at this juncture that Kant combines the two aspects in his
description – or summary – of the Epicurean position, namely (*a*) that there
is no limit in our investigation of appearances; to put it cognitively, that
there is nothing beyond the sphere of appearances which can pretend to be
the subject matter of our enquiry. (*b*) Kant concurrently gives the Epicurean
position a substantive innuendo when he refers to the beginning of the world
as a concern or subject matter which lies beyond the field of appearances.
The notion of the beginning of the world is a trans-empirical notion *par*
excellence and thus has to be disregarded once we cling to the sphere of
appearance, and once we assume that, in the terms of that sphere, there is
no cognitive limit and no substantive beginning of the world. Hence events
as investigated and encountered within the scope of appearance, are deter-

mined by unalterable laws of nature. Here again, once we emphasize the immanence of the laws of nature, there is no reason to assume a cause distinct from the world or from nature. The notion of the cause corresponds to the notion of the beginning of the world, while the notion of the field of appearances corresponds to the notion of the immanent laws of nature.

Having summed up the Epicurean position, Kant observes that these are very sound principles because they expand the scope of speculative philosophy by enabling us to discover the principles of morality without depending upon non-moral or theoretical sources. Kant hints here at his own system by demarcating the speculative concern from the moral concern. He takes the Epicurean system as a system confined to the theoretical realm; while recommending its soundness in that realm he points out that the principles of morality have to be sought outside the field of appearances which is the proper concern of the Epicurean system only in so far as its theoretical aspect is taken into account. It should be observed that Kant does not mention the moral aspect, the importance of which is obvious in the Epicurean system, in his typological presentation – but deals with it rather extensively in his critical and analytical approaches. Kant also observes that Epicurus encourages and furthers knowledge, but that by doing so he prejudices the practical interest.

On the other hand, Kant observes of Plato that while Plato supplies excellent practical principles, he permits reason to indulge in ideal explanations of natural appearances, with regard to which speculative knowledge is alone possible to us – and that he does so to the neglect of physical investigation. Typologically speaking Epicurus and Plato represent respectively two extremes of the disequilibrium between the practical and theoretical interests of reason: Epicurus is bent on a theoretical enquiry and achieves his end by prejudicing the practical and moral considerations; Plato superimposes the practical principles on reason in general and thus harms the physical or theoretical investigation whose proper subject matter is the sphere of natural appearance, which must be explained immanently. Hence Plato's neglect is a parallel to Epicurus' prejudice. Both systems or types of philosophy are at fault, because each says more than it knows – or oversteps the legitimate boundaries of its legitimate concern: the Epicurean type oversteps the legitimate boundaries of the theoretical by encroaching on the practical; the Platonic approach does not do justice to the theoretical in the sense delineated by Kant, where the theoretical concern is limited to appearances and has to explain them through unalterable laws of nature which are laws of the phenomenal world and are not to be derived from the noumenal world.[1]

---

[1] *Kr.d.r.V.*, B, p. 499–500; Kemp Smith's transl., p. 427–428.

At this point one might venture to suggest that Kant's system is an attempted synthesis between the Epicurean and the Platonic attitude: an attempt to give to the natural, the phenomenal and the theoretical their due and to give the trans-empirical, noumenal and intellectual theirs too. One might add, still within the typological context, what Kant says in his Logic, namely that although the Epicurean school could never achieve the reputation the Stoic school achieved, there is one thing to be said for the Epicureans, – that they were the best philosophers of nature of all the Greek thinkers.[2] The term "philosophers of nature" here, probably, connotes the philosophers concerned with nature in the immanent sense – a position defined elsewhere by Kant as an Epicurean position to which they clung without any limitation, namely that everything in the totality of the world occurs according to the order of nature.[3]

There is another aspect to the clash between Epicurus and Plato within the typological context which is obviously related to the previous one: Kant's distinction between sensualists and intellectualists. Epicurus may be regarded as the outstanding philosopher among the sensualists, while Plato is the outstanding philosopher among the intellectualists. The sensualists maintain that reality is to be found solely in the objects of the senses, and consequently that all else is fiction. The intellectualists on the other hand declare that the senses are nothing but an illusion, and that the understanding alone knows what is true. The sensualists did not, to be sure, deny the concepts of understanding of reality, but they considered these concepts merely as logical or, to put it differently, merely as formal. In Kant's words, they admitted intellectual concepts but only sensible objects. It is clear from this that the emphasis of the sensualist approach coincides with the previous description of the Epicurean system as confined to the field of appearances. Plato who represents the intellectualists required that true objects be purely intelligible. We approach those objects by means of pure understanding and are thus in possession of an intuition unaccompanied by the senses. The senses, according to the intellectualists, only confuse the understanding in the strict sense of the term.[4] Obviously here too the denial of the senses corresponds to the neglect of the physical, and here, too, it might be suggested that Kant wants to create a new equilibrium – to give the senses their due and to give understanding or reason its due as well. At this point we are

---

[2] Immanuel Kant's *Logik*, 3rd ed., Leipzig, Felix Meiner, 1920, p. 33.

[3] Über die Form und die Prinzipien der Sinnen – und der Verstandeswelt, in *Immanuel Kants Kleinere Schriften zur Logik und Metaphysik*, 2. Aufl., ed. Karl Vorländer, Zweite Abteilung, Die Schriften von 1766–80, Leipzig, Felix Meiner, n.d. p. 131.

[4] *Kr.d.r.V.*, p. 882; p. 667.

already on the threshold of the critical exposition and, as we shall see, within the critical exposition, the traditional clash between Epicureans and Stoics replaces the dichotomy between Epicureans and Platonists. The ethical element consequently now becomes central.

2

The emphasis placed on sensualism characteristic of Epicurus has an immediate bearing on Kant's evaluation of ethics in the Epicurean system. Indeed, Kant says of Epicurus that he limits his concepts to sensuous objects and to sensuous grounds of determination even when the use of the concept is practical.[5] According to the basic proposition of Kant's system this restriction to sensuality or sensibility has to be rejected *a limine* in so far as the practical interest is concerned. Kant's criticism of the centrality of enjoyment in the Epicurean attitude to ethics enhances his basic rejection of Epicurus. Some observations on the centrality of enjoyment in this context are necessary in order to see their implication for Kant's view and for some problems related to Kant's own systematic position.

It must be observed first that, in so far as the general description of Epicurean ethics is concerned, Kant accepts the popular profile of Epicurean ethics, referring in different ways to what has been described in classical literature as *homo carnalis*. This has to be emphasized for when Kant observes[6] that Epicurus exercised extreme restraint about enjoyment, he is probably hinting at issues in the Epicurean school or tradition namely questions like the relation between enjoyment and freedom from concern, or the intensity of enjoyment which can bring loss of enjoyment in its wake, or variations of enjoyment and the danger of losing what is at hand while searching for variations beyond the reach. But this mitigating statement cannot obliterate the fact that, as a rule, Kant presents Epicurean ethics as centered around *Wohllust, Vergnügen, Genuss,* etc. We therefore have to look into these descriptions more closely since ultimately, as we shall see, Kant's rejection of Epicurean ethics is not a rejection of the problems Epicurus faced, or failed to resolve satisfactorily, but a refusal of the motivation for searching for solutions to these problems.

Epicurus is presented as a philosopher of morality who let virtue be determined by the will only because of the pleasure promised;[7] hence Kant

---

[5] *Kr.d.pr.V.*, p. 162; p. 146.
[6] *Logik*, p. 30.
[7] *Kr.d.pr.V.*, p. 27; p. 23.

says in a letter to Mendelssohn of December 25, 1770, that in Epicurus' view, well-being (*Wohllust*) is not only a *criterium boni* but the *summum bonum*.[8] In so far as what Kant calls "practical material determining grounds in the principle of morality" are concerned, the Epicurean system is a system based on subjective and internal determining grounds. But in Kant's terms, these are physical or physical feelings.[9] The combination of "physical" and "feeling" here indicates sensuality on the one hand and enjoyment or emotional response to one's physical experience on the other. It is in this sense that Kant in his *Logic* describes the Epicureans' approach as one which posits as the highest good a joyous heart which they called "*Wohllust*."[10] When characterizing the Epicurean approach Kant sometimes even uses such pleonastic expressions as a merry enjoyment of life,[11] as though aware that enjoyment as such does not connote the flamboyant quality which he may have wanted to underline. If Epicurus' approach is understood as one of feelings – and indeed Kant sometimes characterized Epicurus as the philosopher of feelings (*Philosoph der Empfindungen*) – then the superimposition of the description „merry" on the state of enjoyment becomes clear.

The location of the ethical attitude on the level of feelings, physical feelings and enjoyment, clearly implies Kant's criticism of the Epicurean system. But at some points Kant's criticism is even more explicit – and here some of Kant's scattered observations are significant, or at least telling. Thus, for instance, Kant states[12] that the Epicurean approach is characterized by lack of moral striving (*sittliche Bestrebung*), even though he is also aware that Epicurus emphasized a motivating or promoting factor in behaviour precisely because he emphasized the urge towards enjoyment. Epicurus wanted to impel man toward virtue;[13] the concomitant psychological advantage is the fact that Epicurus is essentially concerned with self-love; he thus presented an incentive in the direction of virtue which by the same token deprived virtue of its own inner value.[14] Again, since the emphasis is on enjoyment, Epicurus was concerned only with the value of the state of affairs, but ignored totally the inner value of the person. All these descriptions are placed in the context of antithetical comparisons between

---

[8] *Sämtl. Werke*, vol. X, Briefwechsel, p. 114.
[9] *Kr.d.pr.V.*, p. 48; p. 41.
[10] *Logik*, p. 32–33.
[11] *Kr.d.pr.V.*, p. 103; p. 91.
[12] Kants handschriftlicher Nachlass, Bd. VI, *Ges. Schriften Bd. XIX*, ed. Pr. Ak. d. Wiss, Berlin-Leipzig, Walter de Gruyter & Co. 1934, p. 95.
[13] *Bd. XIX*, p. 174ff.
[14] *Bd. XIX*, p. 198.

Epicurus and the Stoa of Zeno; it is in the context of this comparison that Kant says that Epicurean philosophy descended below the nature of man whilst Zeno's rose above it.[15]

Kant indicates the major deficiency of the Epicurean system more elaborately when he makes the distinction between the execution of an act and its evaluation. The execution of an act can indeed be motivated by feelings or an urge for enjoyment, but the evaluation of the act must go beyond the given data, including the psychological data of motivation. Kant is here suggesting a distinction between execution and, what he calls, dejudication.[16] In so far as the empirical human will is concerned, the Epicurean system shows the factual human condition; yet since ethical behaviour oversteps the boundaries of factuality and sensuality, the distinction between incentives and standards must be maintained. The moral standard cannot by any means be immersed in the given psychological incentives of empirical human behaviour.

In one of his various typological or classifying attempts, Kant refers to four ideals or ideas of morality: the Cynics represent the notion of the simplicity of nature; the Epicureans represent the notion of prudence (*Klugheit*); the Stoics that of wisdom; and the Christians that of holiness.[17] It is by no means clear what Kant meant exactly by attributing the idea of prudence or *Klugheit* to the Epicureans: Kant defines *Klugheit* as making use of other people for one's own purposes;[18] if this is so, prudence would amount to the capacity to use the proper means, but, as we have seen in his more systematic expositions of the Epicurean system, the main point made does not relate to meanings but to enjoyment or motivations. Kant does not, as a rule, present Epicurus as concerned with the rules of prudence but rather as showing the subjective grounds for executing one's acts.

In any case, when Kant does refer to Epicurus and his system as a wholly false formulation of the principle of morality, which is happiness, he is not referring to something unique to the Epicurean system. Happiness is a moral ideal in different systems and for that matter in opposite ones. The rejection of happiness as a moral ideal in general *a fortiori* leads to the criticism of the Epicurean approach, which is ultimately only one variation on the theme of happiness. Kant's criticism was probably aimed at the second part of his description of the Epicurean system of morality, namely that the Epicureans had substituted a maxim of arbitrary choice for law, each according to his

[15] *Bd. XIX*, p. 176.
[16] *Bd. XIX*, p. 115ff.
[17] *Kr.d.pr.V.*, p. 147 note; 127 note.
[18] *Anthropologie*, p. 101.

inclination.[19] This point is probably more germane to the general description of prudence, once prudence is related to the choice of means and once the means have to be used according to one's inclinations in the sense that there is no universal law to prescribe what has to be morally pursued. Once *Wohllust* is an ethical ideal, each of us may interpret *Wohllust* according to his inclinations and may concomitantly take advantage of all possible means to achieve his purpose which is sometimes even described by Kant as a good mood (*gute Laune*).[20] It goes without saying that this description is intended to belittle the Epicurean ideal. At this point we may move to the traditional contrast, i.e. to the Stoa.

3

It must be observed that Kant is by and large concerned only with the moral or ethical aspect of the Stoic school. To be sure, he refers to Stoic "speculative philosophy" and describes it as dialectical, but he neither enlarges on what goes under the generic name of speculative philosophy nor explains in what sense he attributes a dialectical mode of thinking to the Stoics. He does not refer to the physics of the Stoa, or to central concepts like God, fate or *logos*. He rather characterizes the Stoics as being concerned with the sublimity and fortitude of the soul and as claiming that once these heights are achieved, one can forego the enjoyments of life. The Stoics have shown the seeds of the most lofty feelings (*erhabenste Gesinnungen*) and in this sense have shown an unusual degree of dignity.[21] In relation to the moral aspect or ideal of the Stoics, Kant refers to the wise man as an ideal, that is to say, a man existing in thought only, which is in complete conformity with the idea of wisdom.[22]

Though Kant is obviously correct in emphasizing the ideal of the wise man and in summing up the guiding principle of the Stoics as one of wisdom (as opposed to the Epicurean ideal of prudence) – we have to be careful in reading his interpretation because the notion of wisdom is ambiguous; Kant, deliberately or not, informs the traditional notion of wisdom with his own interpretation of that generic concept. When Kant uses the term wisdom rather broadly, as for instance in the last sentences of the *Kritik der praktischen Vernunft*,[23] we cannot take exception: here the doctrine of wisdom

[19] *Kr.d.pr.V.*, p. 145; p. 131.
[20] *Bd. XIX*, p. 191.
[21] *Logik*, p. 33.
[22] *Kr.d.r.V.*, B, p. 597; p. 486.
[23] *Kr.d.pr.V.*, p. 188; p. 168.

is understood not merely as what one ought to do but as what should serve as a guide to teachers in laying out the present and past wisdom which everyone should follow and in keeping others from going astray. But if we look more closely at Kant's use of the concept, we cannot be oblivious of the fact that he interprets it according to the systematic direction characteristic of his doctrine in general. For instance, he defines wisdom as the idea of the lawfully perfect practical employment of reason.[24] The emphasis on the practical employment of reason gives it a specifically Kantian connotation; this connotation emerges even more clearly when Kant relates the concept of wisdom to ends or to duties and to the concept of will. All these components of the notion of wisdom remove it from the realm of appearances; to depict the character of the perfectly wise man in a romance is impracticable.[25] The shift of the concept of wisdom to the field of practice, we observe here, is again related to freedom, for in Kant's sense, we are entitled to assume something within the boundaries of the practical employment of reason which we are not entitled to assume in the field of mere speculation. Thus it can be said that even when Kant, as it were, upholds a notion present in the Stoic tradition, he superimposes on that notion not only his own interpretation but also ingredients of his own conceptual framework. Thus it is a moot point whether he is incorporating a Stoic concept into his system or only taking advantage of a generic term and investing it with a connotation which suits the direction of his system.

Since we are discussing Kant's attitude and the Stoa, let us examine another example of it where his particular interpretation becomes rather striking. Kant says that "though one may laugh at the Stoic who in the worst paroxysm of gout cried out: "pain, however thou tormentest me, I will never admit that thou art anything bad (*kakón, malum*)," he was nevertheless right. He felt it was an evil, and he betrayed that in his cry; but that anything morally evil attached to him he had no reason to concede, for the pain did not in the least diminish the worth of his person but only the worth of his condition. A single lie of which he was conscious would have struck down his pride, but pain served only as an occasion for raising it when he was conscious that he had not made himself liable to it by an unrighteous action and thus culpable."[26] Kant is referring here to one of the basic notions of the Stoa, the notion of the *adiaphora* or *indifferentia* and he duly recognizes its importance. One may wonder whether Kant quoted the anecdote he refers to from a text he had, but he could probably also base this on a saying

[24] *Anthropologie*, p. 101.
[25] *Kr.d.r.V.*, B, p. 598; p. 486.
[26] *Kr.d.pr.V.*, p. 71–72; p. 62.

current in the Stoic literature where pain (*dolor*) is not considered as a *malum* and where *dolor* and poverty are not considered as *mala*. Kant reinforced the Stoic notion of *indifferentia* by making a distinction between what he calls "*Übel*" or woe and "*das Böse*" which is evil proper and which cannot thus be attributed to pain but only to an unrighteous action. His own concept of the worth of a person as distinct from the worth of one's condition also comes to the fore here.

At this point one may wonder whether a variation on the notion of *Wert* or worth or value is to be found in Stoic literature. Yet Kant interpreted Stoic *adiaphora* as an indication of the stature of the agent who is not totally immersed in his condition and maintains a distance from the condition. This in turn is either an expression of his worth or a stimulus which leads him to realize his intrinsic worth in his own consciousness and in his attitude. The very distinction between a person and his condition paves the way for investing the person with a moral dimension; that is to say, values are attributed to persons and not to states of affairs. Though we may see this particular presentation as a piece of ingenious interpretation on Kant's part aimed at finding an affinity between his own system and the Stoic view – the affinity is made possible only by bestowing the concept of value on the concept of *indifferentia*.

Although Kant, as we have seen, refers to the notion of wisdom as a Stoic idea, he feels that he is on safer ground when he attributes the notion of virtue to the Stoics.[27] He emphasizes the centrality of virtue because he understands by virtue an attitude or a moral condition characterized by the moral disposition (*Gesinnung*) in conflict.[28] The conflict implied here is obviously that between *indifferentia* and sensuous urges towards satisfaction, enjoyment or even happiness. It is in this sense that virtue is opposed to enjoyment. The Epicureans use the concept of virtue as well, but according to them, as Kant has it, the concept of virtue already lies in the maxim of furthering one's own happiness. Here the difference between the Stoics and the Epicureans becomes central, since for the Stoics the feeling of happiness is already contained in the consciousness of their virtue. According to Kant, the Stoics assert virtue to be the entire highest good; consequently, happiness is only the subject's consciousness of his possession of virtue. The Epicureans again contradict the Stoics here, since according to them happiness is the entire highest good; consequently virtue is only the form of the maxim by which it could be procured, and indeed by the rational use of means.[29] In a sense the Stoic and Epicurean systems respectively present different versions

[27] *Kr.d.pr.V.*, p. 12 note; p. 12 note.
[28] *Ibid.*, p. 99; p. 87.
[29] *Ibid.*, p. 130; p. 116.

of the theme of happiness. According to Kant both extol happiness springing
from the consciousness of virtue above everything else in life. The Epicureans,
as we have already seen, refer to enjoyment as a motive of action, while the
Stoics correctly refuse to follow that line.[30] Kant seems to follow the Stoics,
since he emphasizes that if he is virtuous, a man will certainly not enjoy life
without being conscious of the righteousness of each of his actions. This is
so much the case that favourable fortune and circumstances of a man's life
do not suffice to make him virtuous before he has the high estimation of the
moral worth of his existence which can arise only from the consciousness of
righteousness. But to have such consciousness, we have to presuppose the
person already aware of the whole notion of moral principles, of virtues as
such, as well as the idea of value and worth, in Kant's sense. If we recall
Kant's statement in this context, namely "do that through which thou
becomest worthy to be happy,"[31] we see again that Kant is superimposing
his own interpretation of the relationship between worthiness and happiness
on the Stoics, when he refers to them as giving rules as to how one ought to
become worthy in order to be happy.[32] The notion of dignity becomes
central again when Kant refers the notion of the good mood characteristic
of the Epicurean system as "*gravitätische Würde*,"[33] probably using the
term *gravitas* as it was understood in different locutions, as close to the term
dignitas. It is precisely at this point that Kant's criticism of the Stoa becomes
telling, and we shall now go on to that aspect of Kant's analysis.

An interesting aspect in the scope of Kant's affinity to the Stoic tradition
is apparent in a far-reaching statement about the nature of philosophy or
philosophers: "On account of ... superiority which moral philosophy has
over all other occupations of reason – the ancients in their use of the term
"philosopher" always meant more especially the *moralist;* and even at the
present day we are led by a certain analogy to entitle anyone a philosopher
who appears to exhibit self-control under the guidance of reason, however
limited his knowledge may be."[34] Although the context refers to the two
objects, i.e. nature and freedom, and although the distinction itself does not
conform to the whole problem and direction of the Stoic system, since living
according to nature becomes their moral norm; we can still interpret Kant's
statement as identifying the philosopher with the wise man. One of the major
characteristic features of the wise man is his *sophrosyne* or *temperantia*,

---

[30] *Ibid.*, p. 133; p. 120.
[31] *Kr.d.r.V.*, B, p. 836; p. 638.
[32] *Bd. XIX*, p. 111.
[33] *Ibid.*, p. 191.
[34] *Kr.d.r.V.*, B, p. 868; p. 658.

rendered by Kant as "*Selbstbeherrschung durch Vernunft.*" In a statement which precedes this, Kant deals with the distinction between philosophy and philosophizing. We can only learn to philosophize, he says, because philosophy in the strict sense of the term is a mere idea. This is so until the one true path over ground by the products of sensibility has at least been discovered. Until then we can only exercise the talent of reason in accordance with its universal principles, while reserving the right of reason to investigate, to confirm, or to reject these principles at their very source.[35] Kant seemed to presuppose or to imply that there is more of a possibility of overcoming the non-rational obstacles in the human psyche, like emotions or in the Stoic sense *pathe*, than of overcoming the presence of the sensible data in the sphere of knowledge since to overcome them would ultimately amount to the emptiness of reason and of concepts. While knowledge requires a correlation between data and reason, morality requires that sensuous data (i.e. emotions or inclinations) be overcome – and not that the two components characteristic of knowledge be correlated. From this point of view morality is more open to the exclusiveness of reason than cognition. This is so in a sense by virtue of the definition of these respective fields.

4

Turning to the critical aspect of the Stoic ethical system, it seems apposite to classify Kant's critical points under four main headings which will be presented below in an ascending order. Kant makes the first two points in a neutral mode of analysis; in other words, the critical evaluation is not explicitly stated, but implied, and has to be extricated from the description.

We start with what Kant called the principle of Dietetics (*Prinzip der Diätetik*), and with the fact that he mentions the maxims of *sustine et abstine* in this context. From this point of view, Stoicism not only belongs to practical philosophy inasmuch as it is actually a theory of virtues (*Tugendlehre*), but is also therapeutics (*Heilkunde*).[36] Having used these medical descriptions, Kant felt compelled to qualify them by saying that Stoicism is philosophic dietetic or therapeutic because it attempts to mould men's way of life merely through their power of reason, a power which guides their sensuous feelings by means of a principle which man gives himself. This therefore becomes an internal therapy, juxtaposed with the external therapy which

---

[35] *Ibid.*, p. 866; p. 657.

[36] Der Streit der Fakultäten in drei Abschnitten, *Kants Ges. Schr.*, ed. Königl. Preussische Ak. d. Wiss. *Bd. VII*, Berlin, Georg Reiner, 1917, p. 100–101.

employs corporeal means and uses pharmacy or surgery. This last dietetics or therapeutics is merely empirical and mechanical.

For the sake of the analysis let us disregard the element of the formulation referring to the notion of the principle man gives himself; this is obviously a Kantian version of Stoicism, hinting at the notion of autonomy or self-legislation which is, as we have seen before, at best, a superimposition of Kantian notions on the Stoic text and texture. There is a more substantial issue at stake here. Kant does not overtly criticize the philosophical system as a sum-total of therapeutic rules. But what does he mean by this description of the Stoic system? He is probably referring to the notion of progressing on the road to virtue, a notion which is addressed to those whose wisdom is not perfect, and, who are therefore involved in the progressive steps leading to wisdom as a virtuous state. Kant could refer to what Seneca said, for instance, namely that the approach to the qualities of human happiness is slow, and that in the meantime the path should be pointed out to those who still fall short of perfection but are making progress. Weaker characters need someone to precede them and to say to them avoid this, or do that. Seneca compares this approach to that of doctors and their advice of preparatory processes in eye treatment. Begin with darkness, says Seneca, and then go into half-light, accustoming yourself gradually to the bright light of day. The dietetics or therapeutics amount to an educative moral teaching which is addressed to human beings en route to *sapientia* called *prokopton*.[37] Why did Kant take exception to this moral gradualism, though, and this has to be reiterated, without criticizing it explicitly? The reason, probably, lies in the presupposition that it is the natural human being who can develop or evolve and become a moral character. The whole notion of gradualism presupposes, to use Kantian terms, that there is no chasm between the empirical and the noumenal character, or, put positively, that there is a possibility of continuously moving upward from the natural inclinations to the moral state of affairs. Indeed, Cicero made this point by noting that all appropriate acts arise from the primary natural impulses. Hence wisdom too springs from these natural impulses. We are first introduced to wisdom by these impulses, and wisdom itself then becomes dearer to us than the source from which it has sprung. In this sense the stages of morality are an immanent perfection within the boundaries of human reality. Kant takes exception to this position, though, as we have seen, he does not express this exception when he describes it.

If this conjecture is warranted, we may turn our attention to Kant's

---

[37] Consult: I.G. Kidd, Stoic Intermediates and the End of Man, in *Problems in Stoicism*, edited by A.A. Long, University of London, the Athlone Press, 1971, mainly p. 164ff.

second descriptive-critical characterization of the Stoics. When presenting a chart of the practical material determining grounds of morality, Kant lists the Stoics along with Wolff in the class of those who presented objective determining grounds of morality. "Objective" here refers to man's inner forum – and Kant characterizes this internal forum as perfection. He juxta-poses the notion of perfection with the notion of theological moralists who indicate an external source for the moral principle, i.e. to the will of God.[38]

Again, in what sense is Kant critical of a moral position centered on the notion of perfection? If the previous suggestion is warranted, the criticism of perfection is related to the criticism of the gradual process of improve-ment. Perfection is the consummation of the process; it is the complete state of affairs achieved by an agent given the resources of his behaviour and his aspirations. In one of Kant's aesthetic descriptions or definitions of perfection, he refers to it as consisting in the completeness of anything after its kind (*Vollständigkeit eines jeden Dinges in seiner Art*).[39] The stress must be laid on the notion of "its kind," since this implies that morality is related to hidden-human-potentialities as potentialities within what belongs to "the kind." Their consummation or completeness is the moral stage which combines wisdom, virtue and happiness. Again, since Kant bases his moral philosophy on the distinction between human inclinations, urges and poten-tialities on the one hand, and the moral imperative on the other, he could not assume that a moral state is consummation *qua* perfection. It is perhaps not by chance that Kant prefers the term "destiny" (*Bestimmung*) to the term perfection (*Vollkommenheit*) for man's empirical moral state.

The first two points, subsumed under the heading of Kant's implicit criticism, can be reformulated by saying that Kant criticizes the Stoics for not making provision for the clash between morality and the given human inclinations and urges. And indeed, he says this rather forcibly in a passage which needs to be quoted *in extenso*:

Yet those valiant men (the Stoics) mistook their enemy: for he is not to be sought in the merely undisciplined natural inclinations which present themselves so openly to everyone's consciousness; rather is he, as it were, an invisible foe who screens himself behind reason and is therefore all the more dangerous. They called out *wisdom* against *folly*, which allows itself to be deceived by inclinations through mere carelessness, instead of summoning her against *wickedness* (the wickedness of the human heart), which secretly undermines the disposition with soul-destroying principles.[40]

---

[38] *Kr.d.pr.V.*, p. 48; p. 41.
[39] *Kritik d. Urteilskraft*, § 15; Meredith p. 70.
[40] *Religion*, p. 50.

Kant is making the following point here: in order to present the moral state as the evolved perfection of human nature, the obstacle to the process of perfection has, to some extent, to be upgraded. The obstacle is folly and not wickedness, and folly can perhaps be understood, to use a traditional term, as a *privatio* and not as a *negatio*. Folly makes it difficult to execute a good maxim, while genuine evil consists in this that a man does not *will* to withstand inclinations which tempt him to transgressions. It is therefore this disposition towards evil which is the true enemy of morality or good, not the inhibitions of the undeveloped state of folly. Kant therefore indicts the Stoics of over-optimism about human nature and its inherent potentiality for morality.

When we come to a further criticism of the Stoa which is centered around the concept of *"Schwärmerei"* or self-delusion (translated frequently as "fanaticism" which is not quite apposite) to some extent we find a paradox. Kant defines self-delusion as a deliberate overstepping of the limits of human reason. Moral self-delusion is overstepping of the limits which practical pure reason sets mankind. Stoics are described as philosophers in this context and indeed the strictest of them have created moral self-delusion instead of sober and wise moral discipline.[41] How is this statement of Kant's to be understood? We have seen that in Kant's view morality for the Stoics is the culminating stage of human self-development. But this seems to be precisely the bone of contention. It is a self-delusion to regard morality within the province of given human behaviour, and it is also a self-delusion to assume that human aspirations are satisfied in morality. Morality is the realization of a duty, not an achievement in terms of bringing aspirations and expectations to their fulfillment. The absence of the distinction between fulfillment and subjugation or, to put it differently, the interpretation of morality as fulfillment, is in Kant's view *"eine Schwärmerei."* This point is re-emphasized in Kant's criticism of the Stoic location of happiness. It can already be said now that once morality is conceived as fulfillment, happiness in turn can be conceived as being constituted by morality.

There is a double self-delusion in Stoicism, or perhaps it would be more warranted to say that there are two interlaced delusions which relate to the two ends of human nature and human urges. Stoicism tends to overestimate human nature in two ways: it conceives of human nature, as we have seen, as imbued with a natural-immanent propensity towards virtue; secondly it conceives of human nature as capable of finding its satisfaction *qua* happiness in the very performance of moral deeds or in virtuous life in general.

---

[41] *Kr.d.pr.V.*, p. 100; p. 88–89.

In one of his references to Stoicism Kant says the following: The Stoic ideal is the most correct, pure ideal of morals. Yet *in concreto*, as applied to human nature, it is incorrect. It is correct that we should act according to this idea, but it is false to assume that one *would* ever act accordingly. On the other hand, the ideal of Epicurus is false according to the pure rule of morals and in the theory of moral principles even though it conforms to the greatest extent to the human will.[42] It is at this juncture that we have to come back to the distinction, mentioned before in the context of the exploration of Kant's evaluation of Epicurus, i.e. between the principles of performance or execution and those of evaluation or adjudication. Epicurus has correctly seen the principles of performance which prompt us to action, but he has mistaken them for principles of evaluation of the nature of the action and its moral substance. Zeno, the Stoic, did the reverse by assuming that principles of evaluation are by the same token principles of performance.

But we can go one step further in Kant's analysis and criticism of the Stoa. After all, the Stoa did not present the view that virtues are pursued for their own sake. The Stoa tried to enhance the state of virtue or good life with the element of happiness. On the one hand it referred to self-sufficient morality, but on the other it took self-sufficient morality to amount to happiness; or in Kantian terms, self-approval is full, true happiness (*die Selbstbilligung die ganze wahre Glückseligkeit*).[43] Kant differs at this issue from the Stoic position on two grounds: (a) he is more anxious than the Stoics to delineate the virtuous life or goodness by virtues, without adding the dimension of happiness to virtue. For Kant this would be to overstep the self-sufficiency of virtues from their own immanent position. The Stoics felt as it were that the virtuous life as such cannot do full justice to the goodness of human life. They introduced the component of happiness in order to make virtues totally self-enclosed and rounded, though they could achieve this only by confusing goodness as a quality of performance and actions with happiness as the satisfaction of the agent, or by confusing goodness as conformity with human destiny with happiness as the fulfilment of human expectations. (b) In order to preserve the purity of goodness Kant was led to maintain a line of demarcation between being worthy of happiness, which is a position achieved within the boundaries of morality, and happiness proper which is an achievement or a state of affairs and as such transcends the boundaries of morality in the strict sense of the term. Self-delusion here amounts to the assumption that the pursuit of goodness is *ipso facto* the pursuit of happiness – and moreover that the realization of

---

[42] *Nachlass, Bd. XIX*, p. 106–107.
[43] *Ibid.*, p. 115.

goodness is *ipso facto* the achievement of happiness. This is an overesti-
mation of human nature, since it assumes that satisfaction can be found in
doing one's duty, and it is conversely an underestimation of the import of
human urges, since there is no reason to assume that human urges will be
erased or elevated and cease to drive towards happiness because their drive
has been shifted to the realization of goodness. "The Stoics ... had chosen
their supreme practical principle, virtue, quite correctly as the condition
of the highest good. But as they imagined the degree of virtue which is
required for its pure law as completely attainable in this life, they not only
exaggerated the moral capacity of man, under the name of "sage," beyond
all the limits of his nature, making it into something which is contradicted
by all our knowledge of men; they also refused to accept the second component of the highest good, i.e. happiness, as a special object of human desire.
Rather, they made their sage, like a god in the consciousness of the excellence of his person, wholly independent of nature (as regards his own
contentment), exposing him to the evils of life but not subjecting him to
them ... Thus they really left out of the highest good the second element
(personal happiness), since they placed the highest good only in acting and
in contentment with one's own personal worth, including it in the consciousness of moral character. But the voice of their own nature could have
sufficiently refuted this."[44] By the logic of Kant's own system as well as by
his assessment of human nature Kant paradoxically appears here as a
protagonist of happiness as an independent or semi-independent component
of the highest good. Since morality proper can lead us only to the threshold
of happiness, namely to worthiness of attaining happiness, happiness supp-
lements morality and worthiness without being included in them. Parallel
to this consideration, human nature cannot forego its aspiration and expectation that the *summum bonum* contains both morality and happiness or,
put differently, the expectation that the worthiness to achieve happiness
will be met in fact too, i.e. that there will be a reward for morality in happiness. The two lines of Kant's reflection on morality meet at this point: The
purity of morality has to be maintained, but happiness has to be retained
as the expectation of the moral person, or – terminologically – on the level
of postulates but not within the orbit of achievement. It is for this reason
that, by separating happiness from virtues, Kant relegated the achievement
of happiness beyond morality, lodging it in the harmonious state of affairs
in which the moral agent finds the fulfilment of his pre-moral or a-moral
urges and expectations: the moral person will be rewarded.

[44] *Kr.d.pr.V.*, p. 145–146; p. 131–132. Consult here the previously mentioned article
by Y. Yovel.

Kant seems to realize the difference between conditions of morality and morality proper, though he differs from Aristotle here. Aristotle indicated that well-being is a necessary condition for the virtuous life. He therefore saw the difference between well-being and virtuous life while still maintaining that the virtuous life depended upon well-being as a state of affairs which was a necessary condition for conforming with virtues and shaping the character in accordance with them. Kant removes well-being from its conditional – or pre-conditional – position for the fulfilment or extension of morality, since only the morally worthy person can expect to enjoy well-being and happiness. The necessary precondition is turned into the to-be-expected supplement. Nevertheless, unlike the Stoics, and in affinity with Aristotle, Kant conceives of happiness as an integral part of the total state of affairs. We must emphasize in this context that the totality of the state of affairs does not only consist of morality in the strict sense but also of happiness. But if this is so, then despite the fact that Kant tried to remove morality from the sphere of human urges into the sphere of pure reason, on the level of pure reason he lets the voice of human nature speak. He appears to represent the needs inherent in human nature which cannot be totally suppressed, or sublimated as we would say nowadays, by placing them on the level of virtues. Kant formulates the duality between reason and nature as representing considerations of principles on the one hand of pure reason and as representing nature on the other. He makes the *summum bonum* consist of both morality and satisfaction in spite of the initial fundamental difference between the two components. If this is so, then from the historical and typological point of view, Kant is torn between two attractions: he is aware of his kinship with the Stoics because they emphasize the self-sufficiency of moral life. But he is also attracted by Epicurus who attempts to render the human urge for happiness as being moral by identifying a virtuous life with a happy life whereas the Stoics identify a happy life with a virtuous life. To some extent Kant is attempting a synthesis between Epicurus and the Stoa – and one of the dilemmas of his system is to be found at this point.[45]

One basic dilemma has to be reiterated: the notion of the Primacy of Practical Reason was meant to refer to solutions of antinomies which are not resolved within the sphere of theoretical reason. But as a matter of fact, and this is one of the results of Kant's teaching, the antinomies do not find

---

[45] On the difference between Kant and the Stoa see the brief but pertinent comment in: A.A. Long, *Hellenistic Philosophy, Stoics, Epicureans, Sceptics*, London, Duckworth, 1974, p. 208.

Consult also the extensive analysis of W. Schinck, Kant und die stoische Ethik, *Kant-Studien*, XVIII, 1913, p. 419–475.

their resolution within practical reason either. To be sure, we have to distinguish here between the idea of freedom which is the foundation of practical reason and identical with it since freedom and spontaneity are synonymous, and the postulates in the limited sense of the term, namely the immortality of the soul and the existence of God. They are postulates proper in that they refer to the fulfilment of practical reason and not to its foundation. Thus they refer to what is beyond practical reason or to a reality demanded for the sake of the moral fulfilment of human expectations. This also applies to the notion of happiness: morality does not contain the achievement of happiness immanently, because it does not contain any aspect of achievement whatsoever. Neither does morality guarantee the achievement. It only, as it were, makes it more warranted *qua* expectation, or ultimately transforms the notion of goodness *qua* principle into the notion of supreme goodness which by definition contains the aspect of happiness. Kant's system therefore appears here as a systematic exercise in deferring: he defers antinomies from theoretical reason to practical reason and again defers the fulfilment of expectations from the sphere of practical reason as founded in freedom to the sphere of postulates, which are expectations formulated from the perspective of morality, but are not an integral part of morality proper.[46]

It is because of this systematic consideration that Kant's continuous references to Epicurus and to the Stoa are of significance – in addition to the fact that they are historically and typologically an interesting aspect of Kant's own discourse.

---

[46] See the present author's: (1) *Experience and Its Systematization, Studies in Kant*, 2nd and enlarged edition, The Hague, Martinus Nijhoff, 1972, p. 111ff. (2) *On The Human Subject, Studies in The Phenomenology of Ethics and Politics*, Springfield, Charles C. Publishers, 1966, p. 134ff. (3) Desire and Spontaneity, *The Review of Metaphysics*, Vol. XXX, No. 1. September 1976, p. 39ff.

NAME INDEX

Aristotle 2, 13, 17, 18, 26, 27, 33f., 39, 40–42, 51, 62, 69f., 71, 72, 93, 94, 95, 121, 122f., 147
St. Augustine 12

Bayle, Pierre 120f.

Campanella, Tommaso 72
Cicero 43, 56, 142
Cynics 136

Epicurus 131f.
Eucken, Rudolf 121

Ferguson, Adam 119f.

Garve, Christian 120
Gogon, Olof 35

Hardie, W.F.R. 28
Hegel, Georg Wilhelm Friedrich 73f.
Herder, Johann Gottfried 100
Humboldt, Wilhelm von 107
Hume, David 103f., 105, 106

Kidd, I.G. 142
Krüger, Gerhard 108

Leibniz, Gottfried Wilhelm 49f.
Long, A.A. 142, 147
Lovejoy, Arthur 6, 118

Mendelssohn, Moses 135
Mill, John Stuart 39–40
Montesquieu, Charles de Secondat, Baron 121
Moog, Willy 76

Nugent, Francis 2

Pascal, Blaise 117
van de Pitte, Frederick P. 108
Plato 19, 33, 131f.
Pope, Alexander 114, 127
Proklos 18

Rehberg, August Wilhelm 30

Sambursky, S. 60
Schiller, Friedrich 62
Schinck, W. 147
Schulz, Eberhard Günter 30
Seneca 142
Shaftesbury, Anthony Ashley Cooper 119
Socrates 13, 33, 39
Spinoza 35f., 40, 42
Stoa 43, 47, 112–113, 128, 131f.

Tetens, Johann Nikolas 68
St. Thomas 2

Virgil 57

Weil, E. 76
Wirschubski, Ch. 56
Wolff, Christian 143
Wolfson, Harvey, Austryn 36
Wolke, Christian Heimes 83

Xenophon 13

Yovel, Yirmiahu 50, 76, 146

Zeno 136, 145

SUBJECT INDEX

relative 49
religion 48f., 96f.
 revealed 97f.
reproduction 101f.
republicanism 66f.
resentment 126
respect 10, 24f., 54f., 111f., 65, 79
response 32, 111f.
responsibility 6
restraint 94
reverence 28f., 115
reward 40f., 146
right, rights 55, 90, 114

sage 146
salvation 37
sapientia 142
satisfaction 32f., 39
schema, schemata 75, 88
schematism 67
schooling 83
Schwärmerei 144
science, sciences 23, 33, 67f.
self-determination 12f.
self-formation 80f.
self-interest 55, 75
self-love 20, 44f., 75f., 124f., 135f.
self-sufficiency 17f.
sensibility, sensuality 2f.
sensualists 133f.
servility 90
sexual attraction 108f.
shame 59
similarity 125
sincerity 129
Sittsamkeit 115f.
skin colour 102f.
society 76
sophrosyne 140f.
soul 33
speculation 24, 132f., 137
spirit 74, 76
spirit of a nation 121
spontaneous 2f., 10, 80f.
state 33f., 63f.
 constitution of 64f.
subject, subjects 2f., 78f.
subjective 49
sublime, sublimity 28f., 54f., 105f.
substance 40
summum bonum 135f., 146f.

sympathia moralis 128
system 119

teacher 88f.
teaching 82f.
teleology 55f., 73f., 103
telos 16f.
temperantia 140
tertium quid 1, 8, 65, 68, 94
theorizing 50
theory 18, 26f., 132f.
therapeutics 141f.
thinking 89f.
thought 34
time 74, 76
totality 51
trust 128f.
"turning the soul" 19f.

unity 8f.
universal society 107f.
universality 17f., 89, 97
unsocial sociability 116f.
urge, urges 22, 120
utilitarianism 38f., 44f., 119
utility 38f., 122f.
utopia 50, 51, 72f.

valor 60
value 138f.
vanity 116f.
veneration 128
veracity 128f.
Verstand 25
vice, vices 94, 114, 121
virtue 7, 28, 71, 91f., 122f., 134f.
vocation 29f.
Volkscharacter 103
Volksgeist 103
Volksseele 103

war 54f.
well-being 128
wickedness 60f., 143
will *passim*
wisdom 23f., 34, 37, 45, 136, 137f.
wise man 137f.
Wohlleben 16
Wohllust 135
work 95
worth, worthiness 47f., 138f., 140f.